John Bellany

BY JOHN MᶜEWEN
with a Foreword by
John Russell

MAINSTREAM
PUBLISHING

EDINBURGH AND LONDON

First published in Great Britain in 1994 by

MAINSTREAM PUBLISHING COMPANY

(EDINBURGH) LTD

7 Albany Street

Edinburgh EH1 3UG   .

ISBN 1 85158 632 6 (cloth)

ISBN 1 85158 689 X (paper)

A catalogue record for this book is available from the British
Library

Designed by James Hutcheson
Typeset in Adobe Garamond by Litho Link Limited,
Welshpool, Powys, Wales
Printed in Singapore by Toppan

John Bellany is represented by Angela Flowers Gallery

Flowers East
199/205 Richmond Road
London E8 3NJ

Telephone 081 985 3333
Fax 081 985 0067

This book is to be returned on or before the last date stamped below.

10 MAR 1995		
31 MAR 1995	-8 SEP 2005	
28 APR 1995	-6 NOV 2008	
18 MAY 1995		
-8 JUN 1995		
19 JUN 1995		
30 JAN 1996		
27 JAN 1997		
17 FEB 1997		
23 NOV 1999		
29 JAN 2002		LIBREX
19 FEB 2002		

Self-Portrait, 1965, oil on board, 180 × 120CM, 72 × 48IN.

Mid Cheshire College

Holiday Opening Times
HARTFORD ONLY
Monday to Thursday
9.15-12.15
1.15-4.45

Friday
9.15 - 12.15
1.15 - 4.15

**Closed at Weekends and Bank
Holidays**

Tel No: 01606 720646
PLEASE RING TO CHECK AVAILABILITY

THE BELLANY FAMILY

ACKNOWLEDGMENTS My thanks above all to John

Bellany, without whom there would be no book, and to Helen, Jonathan, Paul and Anya for all their help; to John and Margaret Bellany, Sandy Moffat, not least for the use of his private letters, and Alan Bold, who has also kindly permitted the inclusion of his fine poem *The Voyage of John Bellany: A Triptych*. Also, in multifarious ways, to Norman Ackroyd, Mary Rose Beaumont, David Brown, Alan Davie, Michael Craig-Martin, Peter de Francia, Joanna Drew, Rosa Esman, William Gear, Wolfgang and Jutta Fischer, Douglas Hall, Jonathan Harvey, Paul Huxley, Bert and Betty Irvin, Monika Kinley, Lorraine McCann, Halima Nalecz, Norman and Jean Reid, Carel Weight and Richard Zeisler. Finally, my special thanks to all concerned at Mainstream Publishing and the Angela Flowers Gallery.

Contents

Foreword

The life story of John Bellany can be unravelled in his art. But it has also been very well told by a painter, Alexander Moffat, and by a poet, Alan Bold, both of whom have kept company with John Bellany since all three of them were students in Edinburgh.

The experience of growing up in true companionship with one's contemporaries is one of the great subjects for the novelist, the poet and the autobiographer. Its interest is perennial. A classic, in this context, is Gustave Flaubert's correspondence with the friends of his youth. Another is William Hazlitt's reminiscences of the Lake Poets. In terms of ardour, and of enduring unselfish affection, Moffat and Bold are of their kin. In terms of intellectual challenge, their relationship with Bellany has always been a trio for equals, even if there were times when John Bellany had to defeat his demons unaided.

And now we have John McEwen's biography to bring us up to date. I must say forthwith that this is a marvellous book. McEwen was born in the same year as Bellany. As a Scotsman from the Borders, he is close enough to Bellany's Edinburgh to know what the three of them are talking about. He has spent much of his life in the art world – primarily in London, but with many a foray elsewhere – and he knows on what terms Bellany has had to work for professional survival. (His medical survival is another matter, but one as to which McEwen has no lack of first-hand evidence on which to draw.)

But John McEwen is not so close to his subject as to be tempted to colorize what is best left in black and white, or to chip in with ideas or fancies of his own. Nor does he presume to second-guess, or to improve upon, the memories of those who were there at the time. He participates, and with a full heart, but he does not intrude. It may even be construed as an advantage that, as he says, he did not meet Bellany until the late 1970s and did not begin to write on him until the mid-1980s. In any case, this is as good a monograph of a painter still with us as we are ever likely to read.

John Bellany always wanted to be a painter, and he saw no reason to set any limit to his ambitions. But what kind of a painter was he to be? He came from a fishing family and a fishing village, at a time when fishing was a high-risk occupation and a fishing village was a compact, close-knit society, complete

With John McEwen, Edinburgh, 1994

unto itself. As Carel Weight said when he was Bellany's professor at the Royal College of Art in London, 'He has tremendous roots'.

In his native village of Port Seton, ten miles east of Edinburgh, the boat was not just a professional convenience. It was the ark of life, and the thing on which all else depended. Boats and boat-building were bred into Bellany's father on both sides of his family. He had gone to sea at fourteen. In the Second World War he had risked his life over and over again, using his own boat to explode enemy mines not far from home. Later, he built boats himself, and he also built model boats that were small marvels of accuracy.

Every last timber of the fishing-boats, every last ingrained superstition among the crew, every last puritanical Sunday on shore in adolescence was a part of Bellany's roots. So were the murderous tantrums of the sea, the gutting and smoking of the catch, the sacramental importance of everything that had to do with the job, and the love of home. In the familiar faces all around him in the village, he monitored the phases of life, one by one. All these things went deep with Bellany, as did the camaraderie, the sense of everyone being in it together and the rapid-fire of the conversations on the local bus. There were other, less immediate, things that worked upon his imagination – echoes of what prompted Robert Louis Stevenson to start work on *Treasure Island*, for instance – but fundamentally Port Seton was the whole of life to him. His was on every level an immense inheritance, and one of a kind that our century has worked hard to abolish.

What to do with that inheritance, in terms of art? When Bellany won first prize in a children's art competition arranged by BBC Television, he was clearly very gifted. But children's art has little or nothing to do with the profession of art. When John Bellany went to the Edinburgh College of Art as the first student from Port Seton ever to be accepted there, it was for him to make himself.

Bellany was sometimes what is called a troublesome student. But this did not prove a handicap. Throughout his eight years (1960–68) as a student and graduate student, first in Edinburgh and later in London, he had successes that consistently nurtured his development.

He never got spoilt, either. On early visits to London, he and his friends would sleep in shop doorways to save money, and I would lay money on his doing it again if he had to. He had remarkable teachers, both in Edinburgh and in London. Not one of them painted in a way remotely akin to his own. Nor did they ever suggest that he should paint nice pictures for nice people. They got him out of scrapes. They talked to him in ways that made perfect sense and were never patronising.

They made it possible for him to travel to Paris, to Holland and to Belgium and then, on an official visit in 1967, to what was then East Germany. And he put all this to maximum advantage. It did not make him a careerist who went around shopping for galleries and collectors and museum exhibitions. Even less did it sever him from his Scottish roots. But it gave him a sense of what had been done in great painting, and of what it was like to live in countries that had been taken apart and were not yet together again.

As to what came of all this, it is not for me to pre-empt, and still less to rival, John McEwen's account. The only exhibitions by John Bellany that I have ever seen are the ones that he has had in New York. What struck me at that time was the sheer abundance of the material in each painting. It was as if the ideas were spilling out all over, the way (on a good day) fish spill out of the nets. It was not that they caused congestion, but that space was making room for them, even if it had to be turned inside out, like a glove, or pulled this way or that, as if elasticised. Moreover, each painting was like a high drama in which there were no small parts.

They were paintings that carried more meanings than could be deciphered at any one time. Fancy-dress co-existed with passages that could not have been more down-to-earth. There were recurrent images, and there were others that made a single cameo appearance to hallucinatory effect. Where did they all come from?

Max Beckmann was most people's guess, and of course it was known that Bellany had seen his great show at the Tate in 1965. I happen to think that Beckmann made some of the greatest images in western art, and there is undeniably a mysterious cousinship between some of those images and some of Bellany's. Beckmann's *Journey on the Fish* (1934), *Prometheus* (1942) and *Fisherwomen* (1948) are tremendous images, but they are conceived in terms of monumentality. Bellany in paint is by contrast a conjurer in space, a forester whose woodlands outpace Dunsinane, and a consummate gamesman who gets to reposition the goalposts a hundred times over. He is also a cryptographer, whereas Beckmann explains himself plainly, massively and unanswerably.

We also have to remember that in painting, as in life, John Bellany can be one of the funniest people around. A favourite of mine, in reproduction, is the painting of 1983 called *Only an Emu Passing By*. It related to his visit to Australia, when he was made welcome one evening in true Down-Under style. Waking up and feeling in terrible shape, he looked out of the window and saw an unbelievably bizarre bird just a few feet away. Was he hallucinating? Going right round the bend? 'Not at all,' said his host. 'That was only an emu passing by.'

On this and other occasions, when it seems that it is not in his nature to discard anything whatever as potential picture-material, I also remember that Bellany was much impressed by the Oskar Kokoschka retrospective at the Tate in 1982. Kokoschka, too, could derive a wild humour from incidents that might

Only an Emu Passing By, 1983, oil on canvas, 173 × 152.5CM, 68 × 60IN.
(Collection Susan Kasen Summer and Robert D. Summer)

Bethel, 1967, oil on board, 248 × 319.7CM, 97½ × 125½IN. (Southampton City Art Gallery)

prompt in others a moment of self-pity. In his *Time, Gentlemen, Please* (1971–72) he is seen to walk, not quite steadily, out of a well-lit London pub in which the classic call to get up and go is being heard. If we happen to know that Kokoschka was at that time in his eighty-sixth year, we may wonder how many more times he would live to hear that ancient formula.

As readers of this book will discover, Bellany came face to face with death at a much earlier age than Kokoschka and told it to go away and not come back in a hurry. Hardly was he off the operating table than he was back at work again. In short order, new opportunities came to him, and new ideas, too. The Fitzwilliam Museum in Cambridge fostered an exhibition in which homage was paid to Port Seton, as well as to Titian and the Coleridge of *The Ancient Mariner*.

The British Council could hardly have found a better use for its money than when it sent him and his wife to Prague, Vienna and Budapest for six months in 1993. What came out of those months showed him as, once again, the archetypal concerned European. What was to become of these great cities in a future which, though long hoped for, was not turning out entirely well?

Wherever questions of that kind will be asked, John Bellany will have some challenging answers. Long may he be around to give them, and long may he have at his side Helen Bellany, who has already her place among the great company of artists' wives.

John Russell,
New York,
1994.

The Star of Bethlehem, 1965/66, oil on board, 183 × 244CM, 72 × 96IN. (Tate Gallery, London)

Prologue

J ohn Bellany has as strange a story to tell as any painter and his talent has been the match of it. This may sound a bit florid, but what other western artist in the second half of the twentieth century was brought up in a society that could well be described as medieval? And what other has 'drowned' – in the sense of surviving a liver transplant – and told the tale? John Bellany is the son of a fisherman, a child of the sea, and his art is true to that inheritance.

To say Bellany is unique is merely to acknowledge that he has succeeded; but he has an advantage in that his subject is also unique. Many artists have colonised fishing ports but he was born in one. He paints a common subject with uncommon knowledge.

Man has always had three means of survival: hunting, farming and mining. All three are elemental tasks, filled with uncertainty and terror; but fishing, the hunting of fish, especially. The terror is bravely unspoken but always there. In Bellany's youth, when his father was a skipper, the boats were much smaller. The men worked on open decks and fundamentally the way things were done had not changed for centuries. So they believed in God and trusted in luck, which made them deeply superstitious; and because they believed in God they also believed in hell. Working on the sea they knew God's wrath like no one else and they also knew the devil's work. Once Bellany whistled on a boat. The crew were shocked. They feared he might have whistled up a storm. So he was brought up in a world where superstition was a matter of life and death and where each new week might be the last for his father and the men of the village.

There were more churches than pubs in Port Seton but the population's dependence on both was grounded in fear and, of course, hope. The *Good Hope* is one of the many boats Bellany has depicted. The names are beautiful: the *June Rose*, the *Harvest Queen*, the *Star of Bethlehem*. They are steeped in meaning like all poetry, and play a prominent role in his art.

To be taken on a tour of the harbour by John Bellany is a revelation.[1] Boats have always been his obsession and it was through drawing them that he trained his eye and hand. This was his artistic

Three Fishers, 1966, oil on board, 218 × 213.5CM, 85¾ × 84IN.

launching and their symbolic importance has become as vital to him as their physical capability was to his father. His father was also a boatbuilder, so Bellany has known them inside-out from his earliest years. The boat is an archetypal symbol for him: the barque of life. Life is often seen as a voyage but the metaphor is particularly appropriate in Bellany's case, as the poem on page 20 by his friend Alan Bold movingly celebrates.

With Alan Davie, 1990

When he was a boy John Bellany went to church three times every Sunday – morning, afternoon and evening. He no longer attends but wryly admits, in the words of Brendan Behan, that 'it's easy to be a daylight atheist'. Sandy Moffat, his oldest and closest artistic friend, is categorical in saying that Bellany's art is 'deeply imbued with religious feeling'. Bellany is an expressionist, that modern form of romanticism. His art is about death and redemption; just as art outlives the artist so the soul outlives the body.

John Bellany is also a Scot, a distinction which means nothing outside Britain but a great deal within it. The Celts can be tiresomely self-assertive but they are peculiarly tribal, mythologically inclined and certainly, in the case of the Scots, genealogically obsessed. Romanticism was as Scottish as it was German in its origins, and it is only strange that it took so long for Scotland to produce an expressionist painter of the international stature of Alan Davie. 'People used to ask me why I didn't paint in a Scottish tradition,' Davie recalls. 'I said, what Scottish tradition? It's all French. Very few Scottish painters have been true to their Celtic origins.' Davie is one of these and he acknowledges Bellany, 'a painter of Nordic mystical power', as another. 'At his best I think he's one of the great masters of our time – no doubt about it,' Davie affirms.

Davie was one of Bellany's first local heroes. Another was the poet Hugh MacDiarmid, a founder of Scottish Nationalism who called for 'giantism' in the arts. 'John lived his life in terms of heroes,' says Alan Bold. To have heroes is also a Celtic trait, an essential ingredient of mythology. Homer's heroes put to sea, as did John's father and the men of Port Seton and Eyemouth. John confronted art in the same spirit: as a Calvinist, driven by the moral imperative of work, and a Scotsman, with the traditional pride in his birthright.

Only a Scot knows the fury of that pride, which finds its spur in defiance of the English, the 'auld enemy'; Goliath to Scotland's David. When the English scored a goal against the Scots at Hampden, Bill Shankly, a full-back for Scotland that day, said the silence of the 140,000 crowd was so total he could hear the patter of the raindrops as the ball shook the back of the net. And yet, as so often happens with Scots, the English have done Bellany proud: from the support he received as a student at the Royal College of Art to John Russell's foreword to this book.

John Bellany has always seen the wider world as his stage. He has no false modesty. He aspired to be a hero from the start, as was proudly proclaimed by the scale of the paintings he exhibited on the railings outside the National Gallery in Edinburgh as a student; in Davie's words they were already works of 'tremendous spiritual and dramatic power'. For many these grim, visionary testimonies to the stoicism of the fishing life have a metaphorical force he has never surpassed, linking him with that proud tradition of Scottish art, exemplified by Burns and Scott, which honours the courage and dignity of working people.

His own stoicism has been no less of an anchor. He has suffered more trials and indignities, the worse for being self-inflicted, than most men, and always managed to turn them to his advantage. He has painted from the depths of despair and in order to numb physical pain; but he has always 'soldiered on', in Julian Spalding's words, 'through an age when so many artists forgot that art was about feeling and tried to feebly distance it from life and real experience'.[2]

This book is intended to be a log of John Bellany's voyage so far. It is also a retrospective of his art. Expressionism is a Nordic tendency and Bellany's art is closer to German, Flemish and Dutch painting. The English find expressionism distasteful on the whole; when it came to the crunch the British Council preferred to promote Henry Moore rather than Francis Bacon – but it is Bacon's reputation which now stands higher. Bellany's recognition has been considerable but in England he remains, like Davie before him, part of an alien tradition.

As a Scottish art critic born in the Borders the same summer as John Bellany, I am ashamed not to have written about him until the mid-1980s. I hope, if I had known then what I know now – the profound spirituality and at times raw power of his painting – I should have acted more wisely. But the fact is – and this says something about life in a metropolis – I do not remember meeting him until the late 1970s. It is only through accepting his invitation to write this book that I have fully understood his achievement.

There has been a change of attitude to death and religion in the last fifty years more profound than at any other time in history. Science is responsible, in fishing as in everything else. It is an 'industry' today, the new boats satisfying a different set of contingencies and beliefs. The artist's cousin, also called John Bellany, is a fisherman aboard the *Bonaventure*, which is twice the size of John's father's *Queen of the Fleet*. It looks enormous in port, like a mini-ferry – an 'incredible hulk', Bellany calls it. Made of steel, it is not at one with nature the way the old 'bonny' wooden boats of his childhood were. It defies nature. It has a covered deck, bunks, shower, refrigeration, radar, telephone and television.

The boats have changed and so has the life of Port Seton. His cousin's children work in the service industry. The processions and feasts have been replaced by children's galas. Everyone has a car and shops at the superstore. The closed, secretive community has been blown apart. Visitors to Port Seton used to be disparagingly referred to as 'strangers'; and you could be a 'stranger' if you lived there a lifetime. Now everyone is a stranger to everyone else and even the crews commute.

Bellany's Breughel-like commemorations of old Port Seton seemed dated to the point of eccentricity in the days of Pop Art. His trendy fellow students at the Royal College scoffed at their parochialism. But who looks dated in 1994, with a medieval war raging in Bosnia and God replacing the Bomb? Bellany is currently painting the consequences in Eastern Europe of these upheavals. No artist is better equipped to empathise with this theme of roots and rootlessness; with life as a voyage from past to present, between the devil and the deep.

John Bellany's cousin, also named John Bellany, with John McEwen and the artist, March 1994. The model fishing-boat was made by Dick Bellany

THE VOYAGE OF JOHN BELLANY: A TRIPTYCH

The curves that hold the earth together speak
A language of their own, a tone defines
An area of understanding: lines
Control emotions as the colours break

The barriers between the talk and look
Of life. A vision in the distance shines
And comes much closer with its great designs
On you. You look much harder as you take

The vision in. You recognise the folk,
You know the feeling, what the artist means,
Or think you do until the stunning scenes
Knock back your senses to a state of shock.

You die the day you see your own death.
You succumb to the ultimate and avoidable defeat.
You see the contours of your face
As fraudulent and you know you're done.
You cling on to moments of solace,
Stand staring at the setting sun,
Which only reminds you
That everything ends,
Even the earth that nourished you.
It's all a great whirl,
A dance with frequent interruptions—
Taps on the shoulder, challenges.
Changes of tempo, stumbles—
And you cannot keep going forever
You feel.
You cry halt, but nobody listens.
Nobody cares.
The earth shrugs its shoulders,

Turns over for a goodnight's sleep,
And wakes up without you.
Others open their eyes,
Waiting for you,
And look around.
The sky decides between grey and green
And blue and black.
There are births,
There are ancient animal cries.
Only you aren't there to hear them.
You have vanished.
It is accepted as a fact of life.
Nobody is astonished.
But then the sea swells, the earth shrinks,
And somebody sees things differently
And you come back.
You want to come back.

The art of exploration looks at places
Nobody has yet explored for fear
Of finding out too much and so we stare
Alarmed, alone, before the frontal faces

That probe our posture as a human species.
The eyes would seem to have it: see, they glare
And glow and catch our frantic glances where
They look beyond the painted surfaces.

The voyage is in motion, how the seas
Turn over, how the earth is insecure,
How much anguish going from here to there:
This journey over endless ecstasies.

Alan Bold.

CHAPTER I

Summer of '42

In the sixteenth century there was much trading between Italy and the North Sea ports. One of these was Prestonpans and The Saltpans near Cockenzie. Bellany has always fantasised that a certain Venetian artist came on one of these trips and sired a new line of which he is a descendant – not Giovanni Bellini but John Bellany! It adds significance to Sandy Moffat's memory of his friend painting 'a magnificent transcription of Poussin's copy of Bellini's *The Feast of the Gods* when an art student in Edinburgh'.[3]

How long the Bellany clan have been a fishing family remains a mystery but in the artist's case it is entrenched on both sides. His grandfather was the captain of a boat at Port Seton and married a daughter of the Weatherhead family, the most famous boatbuilders on the Berwickshire coast; his father, Dick Bellany, went to sea at fourteen and eventually owned his own boat. Dick Bellany married Nancy Maltman, daughter of a famous fishing family from Eyemouth, forty miles south of Port Seton. The most renowned of the Maltmans was Tarry, a cousin of John's great-grandfather, who was once brought back to life five hours after being pronounced 'dead' from drowning – a Jonah-like rebirth which John has since emulated when he had an eight-hour liver transplant operation.

John Bellany was born on 18 June 1942 at 18 Gosford Road, Port Seton. His father was away on active service in the war. The departure of the men precipitated births in 1942 in the same way that their post-war return did in 1947. His sister Margaret arrived on the 1947 wave.

The war caused friction in Port Seton between the members of the Closed Brethren, a stricter version of the low church Plymouth Brethren, and the rest of the town, who were Presbyterians. The Brethren, being pacifists, conscientiously objected to military service and were able to continue fishing while the rest of the community joined up. Dick Bellany had joined the Naval Reserve, one of a gallant band of sea captains who volunteered to use their boats as mine-sweepers in the Firth of Forth. The mines were detonated by the percussive effect of the boats' propellers. Several of the Port Seton boats and their crews were lost on these virtual suicide missions, and Dick – as Second Hand R.W. Bellany RNPS – was

John Bellany as a baby

Dick Bellany during the war

Sonnie Maltman, John Bellany's
grandfather, Eyemouth, 1965

John Bellany's mother, Nancy,
1938

Mentioned in Dispatches, 1 July 1941, for his part in the operations. At the time of his son's birth, he was a petty officer with the Royal Navy in the Indian Ocean and Ceylon, where he spent the rest of the war. He did not return until the demob in 1945.

John Bellany's earliest memories are of Eyemouth, because his mother preferred to stay there with her parents until the war ended. Eyemouth is on the North Sea whereas Port Seton, on the Firth of Forth, lay in the path of the enemy bombers on their raids of the docks at Leith and Rosyth and the vital communications link of the Forth Bridge.

'My childhood was idyllic. There were no strictures. It was all high romance, lyrical. There was none of the brutality that seems to have entered the world of children today. Love was the great thing. My Maltman grandparents epitomised the absolute basis of the Christian spirit: "To give is better than to receive". They really were the salt of the earth. So were my Port Seton grandparents but there was never the same intimacy, perhaps because I did not see so much of them in those first years. But the camaraderie was absolutely fantastic. Everybody knew each other, their cousins and parents and all about them. I think that that's what's gone wrong with the world. We've all become far too removed from each other.'

Locally, the surname Maltman was abbreviated to 'Mat', so his grandfather was Sonnie (short for Alexander) Mat. Sonnie was born in 1881 – the year of the Eyemouth Disaster, which his father survived, when 129 Eyemouth fishermen lost their lives in one day in a tremendous storm[4] – and was still the captain of a boat, the *Margarets*. The Maltmans lived at 4 Home Street, their neighbours the skippers of boats whose names are now familiar from Bellany paintings: the *Bethel*, *Good Hope* and *Adoration*.

Eyemouth has always been a focal point of the east-coast fishing industry. It has the largest harbour, a fish-market and the bigger of the two boatbuilding yards, the smaller being in Port Seton. Boats from ports along the Fife coast, like Pittenweem and Anstruther, as well as from Port Seton, Fisherrow and Dunbar on the southern shore of the Forth, land their catches there through the week and sail home at weekends. Not surprisingly, intermarriage between the families of the fishing villages is commonplace.

When Dick Bellany was demobbed in 1945 he stayed in Eyemouth with the Maltmans, his Uncle William giving him a job at Weatherhead's where they were building the *Mizpah*, destined to be one of the best boats on the east coast for many years, and later a name of great symbolic significance to John Bellany. The Weatherheads had always been boatbuilders and the talent was inherited by Dick Bellany, an expert maker of model boats. He never used kits but carved from wood, making the details from ingeniously recycled bric-à-brac. They remain his son's proudest possessions and he included his father's model of the *Bounteous Sea* in his 1986 retrospective at the Scottish National Gallery of Modern Art. He assigns the more poetic and imaginative side of his character to his mother and her female Maltman relations, who were great readers. But behind it all is an intense love of home, of the life, security and pride of Port Seton and Eyemouth, of the Borders and Scotland. As Carel Weight, his professor at the Royal College, says with a certain awe: 'John has tremendous roots.'

Eyemouth is more beautiful than Port Seton. It lies on the Berwickshire coast round the headland from St Abbs, a name known the world over from the BBC's shipping forecast; the more sheltered Port Seton, tucked away in the Firth of Forth, in contrast, is today dominated by a power station and is an industrial suburb of Edinburgh. Eyemouth is far more elemental, with its cliff to one side and the bay opening directly on to the North Sea, the town taking the full force of any easterly storm.

John Bellany's grandfather and grandmother, Eyemouth, 1965

'The harbour was packed with all these wonderful different types of boats. That's when I first started drawing, when I was three or four years old; and they were like portraits, except they were of boats rather than of people. I think the focusing and sharpening of the eyes, the synchronisation of hand to eye, started away back at the age of four. I'd draw by the harbour because at Eyemouth the harbour comes right up through the centre of town, so visually it's just staggering. I still think it's one of the most beautiful places in the world. All that colour, all that hustle and bustle of activity, that was the core of my life in both Port Seton and Eyemouth in these days; but it was Eyemouth where it started.'

His grandfather's boat, the *Margarets*, was a forty-footer, a size that would normally put to sea for a day at a time. At Eyemouth the jagged Hurkur Rocks in the bay have to be negotiated before the boats turn into the long harbour formed from the mouth of the River Eye. Old men sat gossiping and reminiscing and families gathered on the seafront, especially if the weather was bad, to watch this hazardous manoeuvre.

In front of the memorial for the Eyemouth disaster in Eyemouth cemetery. Bellany's grandparents' house is in the background

'You got to recognise each boat from the horizon line, and that was heightening your powers of observation because you could only tell by the rigging. So you came to recognise the dominant features and, of course, when it came to drawing them it was like synthesising.'

Even as a child Bellany never considered being anything other than an artist. 'We used to joke about it, say he would end up living on bread and cheese in a garret. But he was in earnest,' his mother told Alan Bold.[5] There was no precedent for such a choice in Port Seton, although his Bellany grandfather had commissioned pictures of his and her sons' boats from a professional artist.

The young John drew boats obsessively, just as his father made them, the two in friendly competition: 'I'd show what I'd been doing to my Dad and he'd say: "Nothing like it! The masts are wrong, you haven't got any cross-beams in that." It was intelligent, constructive criticism because he was

Dick Bellany, skipper of his father's drifter, the *Violet*, 1934

John Bellany's father at 'the fishing' in the 1930s on his own boat, *Queen of the Fleet*. Dick Bellany is second from the left

John Bellany, age 6

With his sister, Margaret

trying to master the same problems himself in his model-making. And at that age it just makes you try harder, makes you look harder. And I'd try and get my own back. I'd see if I could fox him. He'd say: "The derrick's on the wrong side." And I'd say: "You haven't looked. They've changed that." And if I was right I'd be one up. So this kind of banter went on. Whereas my grandmother and the women would say, "Oh, it's really good, son!" about whatever I did, giving encouragement. I could do a line drawing of a boat and get a perfect likeness – an almost Holbeinesque likeness! – at the age of five.

'I always remember there was this ledger with feint ruled lines I used as a drawing book, and across the middle pages I'd drawn a picture of a big drifter called the *Adoration*, the biggest boat in the harbour – it was ninety feet and owned by the skipper who lived two doors away from my grandparents in Home Street. So my little brain had obviously worked this out because I'd run the *Adoration* across two pages – it was centre-spread! – whereas I'd just given a single page to my Grandpa's boat, the *Margarets*, because it was smaller. Of course the *Mizpah*, which my Dad had built, that got a double page and all the accoutrements because I was as proud of my Dad building that boat as somebody would be on Clydeside of their father building the *Queen Mary*. The world for me was in that one place. So that intensity went in and I think that has lingered over the years.'

Danger increased that intensity. Dread of death was forcibly impressed on him in Eyemouth by the graveyard behind Home Street. In his childhood it was a wasteland, a haunting place, where fetching a football was a frightening ordeal: 'Talk about death – I had it right there at my bedroom window!' Death has remained the central preoccupation of all his painting, and perhaps even his phobia for rats – creatures of his worst nightmares – may spring from that view over the wall; although rats are also infamous for leaving sinking ships.

The gravestones have now been removed and the yard turned into a garden, with a monument to the dead of the Eyemouth Disaster and the two World Wars; but the Watchhouse remains, a squat building in the corner of the graveyard lined on the outside with seventeenth-century gravestones.[6] The stones are very worn but their luridly detailed carvings of skulls and bones, presented slab by slab, greatly exercised the young Bellany's imagination. It is to them that he attributes his liking for the diptych and triptych forms.

No doubt the imagery of the stones was made more frightening by the immanence of death in ordinary life. 'People were always getting drowned. There was always that dread. You'd listen to the weather forecast and if there was a force-eight gale neighbours would be out asking: "Is such and such a boat in?" "No, it's not back yet." "Oh, we were expecting them in at six and now it's ten. Has anyone tell't his wife?" In those days the boats didn't have radios – that didn't come in till the 1950s – so all

The Gatehouse, the old cemetery, Eyemouth, adjacent to John Bellany's grandparents' house, where the artist spent much of his childhood

news was by word-of-mouth. People would gather on the seafront and spot the lights on the horizon. They still had to navigate the Hurkurs but when they got past them it was absolutely thrilling. Once, just before the Second World War, there was a boat called the *Spes Bona*, which mistook the entrance and ended up right on top of the rocks. In the morning when the tide went out she was still stuck up on high but the crew were all lost. That image was so vivid to me and it's recurred in my painting many, many times. It's the only boat I paint where the mizzen-mast is in front of the wheelhouse, so that's how it's always recognisable. "Aye, you can see it's the *Spes Bona*, you've got that one right, John!" they'd say, because they'd know at a glance. But it wasn't all doom and torture! On a summer day when the boats come back in an evening calm there's no more beautiful sight.'

The constant danger makes fishing communities especially close-knit and independent, bound by religion and prone to superstition. Sonnie Maltman, like all fishermen, honoured the eighth commandment – 'Remember the sabbath day, to keep it holy' – and never went to sea on a Sunday. Superstition in the fishing villages went hand-in-hand with religious conviction. Early one Monday morning Sonnie left to board ship but, unprecedently, soon returned. He had met the Presbyterian minister on his way to the harbour, a terrible omen, and had cancelled the sailing. Ministers or priests are not the only harbingers of bad luck; so are black-and-white dogs, saying 'salmon' instead of 'red fish', or 'nun' instead of 'yachts before the wind'. A woman on board is unlucky in the same way as it is unlucky for miners to see a woman below ground. And whistling, as Bellany once memorably forgot, is forbidden. Superstition had the profoundest effect on his imagination. Almost all his pictures include symbolic omens of good and evil, of animals and birds, with the cards of fate constantly redealt.

Religion was the anchor of the communities. In Port Seton during the 1940s and 1950s a population of four thousand was served by thirteen churches and meeting-houses. Though frequently and explicitly cited in both the Old and New Testaments, reference to the devil is prudently avoided by the clergy of all Christian denominations today.[7] Their congregations would not stomach it. But this was not the case in the 1940s and 1950s. Every Church warned against the fearful consequences of sin; and none more fiercely than the Church of Scotland. The young Bellany was always terrified by his bedtime prayer – 'If I die before I wake, pray the Lord my soul to take' – because to die, if the preachers were right, was to burn forever in the flames of hell. This horror may have faded but not the awe of the unknowable, the unfathomable.

'There's such a difference in the religious observance of the English – apart from maybe the Methodists. It doesn't touch on this heavy soul-searching,' says Margaret Bellany.

'It's the difference between Trollope and James Hogg,' agrees John. 'The deeper it goes in, the better for your soul – so everybody's trying to plumb the depths. It's taken as the most important thing in their whole existence and that moves into secular life as well. We're not just talking about what happens in the church on Sunday but about a person's behaviour the other six days of the week. You don't just turn it on or off like a tap. The depths you feel through religion for everyone in your life – it's not a question of a surface recognition of *vive la politesse*. So the passions can run very high. And it's the same with fun, you do that with extreme conviction as well. There may have been a lot of churches in Port Seton but the pubs were full, too! The sacred and profane go hand-in-hand.'

Port Seton Church

'Yet you were told that everything's best in moderation,' adds Margaret, 'so when you plumb these great depths and hit the great heights, that's not being moderate – therefore that's where you find your *guilt*!'

Like her brother, Margaret has been divorced and is no longer a church-goer. Both were first married in church, but neither has had their children baptised. 'In the late 1960s and early 1970s the climate was not conducive to that kind of caper,' explains Bellany. So does Margaret still find guilt in his pictures? 'Yes – you don't have to look very far for guilt from whence we came.' Something on the shoulder? 'Definitely!'

Sundays throughout John's boyhood were entirely devoted to religion. 'We went to church all the time it seemed,' remembers Margaret, 'and I think the one thing it did teach you was physical discipline, an hour and a half is a long time for a wee one just to sit.'

The Bellanys sat in the front pew of the gallery, which had been their grandfather's seat. Dues were paid for pews, a custom no longer practised; but in those more hierarchical times to be in the best pew meant you were the most important member of the congregation. There was quite a tribe of Bellanys, enough to fill the two front rows, because there were four families of cousins; but it was Dick Bellany who was most assiduous in his duties.

Dick Bellany, like many Scots, was a man of the Book. In a wartime photograph he stands in naval uniform, a bible prominent on the table at his side. He never lectured his children, preferring to quote moral laws. Some of these are engraved on his children's memory like letters in stone. For Margaret it is: 'In whatsoever state I find myself therewith let me be content,' whereas for John Bellany it is the short sharp shock of: 'Be sure your sins will find you out.' There were many more: 'You earn what you receive'; 'You reap what you sow'. These strictures were often repeated in the general conversation of their parents and grandparents, particularly by their Bellany grandmother, 'a great one for quotes'.

Dressed in the obligatory black suit and sober tie, John would attend the Chalmers Memorial

Church for morning service and then go to Sunday School in the afternoon, both at his own church and the meeting-hall of the Brethren, where his Uncle James was a member. Fun and games were strictly forbidden – 'There were Sundays which seemed to last a hundred years'– then, after tea for the entire Bellany family at his grandparents' house at 5 Wemyss Place overlooking the harbour, they would go to the evening service in the Chalmers Memorial Church.

The building made a profound impact on him, timbered inside like a boat, the cross-beams stencilled with a sky-blue pattern of fish. That here was a barque for the spiritual voyage of life was emphasised by the model fishing-boat which surmounted the communion table as the supreme icon of the place. For the Harvest Festival a stupendous heap of fish was shored against the table, for the artist the most memorable sight of the religious year and another image he has frequently used in his painting.

The *Redemption Song Book* was used, with hymns relating to the sea, rather than the Church of Scotland hymnal. The doctrine was Calvinist but specific to the needs of the fishing way of life, the spiritual significance of work and religion interchangeable. This was his favourite service. The boats sailed at midnight, the doom-laden hymns of the *Redemption Song Book* a last reminder of the transience of earthly existence and the dangers of the voyages ahead. The singing raised the roof. As a member of the choir, Bellany's love of music was born of those fervent evenings.

Will your anchor hold in the storms of life?
When the clouds unfurl their wings of strife
When the strong tide lifts, and the cables strain,
Will your anchor shift, or faith remain?

Chorus
We have an anchor that keeps the soul,
Steadfast and sure while the billows roll.
Fastened to the rock which cannot move,
Grounded firm and deep in the Saviour's love.[8]

At Eyemouth Harbour, 1993

A portrait of John Bellany's grandfather, painted when the artist was 15

The Boat Builders, 1962, oil on board, 4 panels, 275 × 484CM, 108¼ × 190½IN.

With his father and one of his models, 1965

CHAPTER 2

Blue Bonnet Days

The family returned to Port Seton in 1947 and the young John Bellany entered Cockenzie primary school. His awe of death was reinforced by a shocking accident. John Arnot, a fellow pupil, slipped from the harbour wall and was drowned. A crowd gathered to watch the boy's uncle, Peter Donaldson, the Pond Master, dive ceaselessly to try and save the child. He had won a gold medal for swimming in the Empire Games but even his prodigious efforts were to no avail. The village was in mourning for weeks.

Port Seton in those days used to have two spectacular public events: the Bonfire and the Box Meeting. The Bonfire was at Hallowe'en, when the oldest boat would ceremoniously be dragged through the town and burned to signal the end of the fishing year. Next day the Box Meeting heralded the start of the new season.

The Box Meeting is the subject of one of Bellany's most ambitious student paintings. The crews marched through the streets to the Auld Kirk, where the boxes containing the deeds of the boats were blessed. The box was then paraded by the relevant crew bearing a banner proclaiming the name of its boat. Afterwards there was dancing in the streets to several pipe and accordion bands, the women dressed in traditional clothes and the men in their seaman's rig of navy-blue guernseys and trousers, followed by supper at Cockenzie House and the Fisherman's Ball at the Pond Hall. Breughel-like revels continued after midnight at the various pubs – most notoriously Jasper's, today called The Thorn Tree. The Box Meeting is another lost tradition. It has been succeeded by a gala day for the children.

Dick Bellany did not fish for long after returning to Port Seton. In 1951 the doctor presented him with an ultimatum: if he continued fishing, it would be at the expense of his wife's health, which was affected by the anxiety she suffered when he was away at sea. He had survived the war and was by this time back at sea aboard the *Dreadnought*. It would have been a hard decision for most men but not for him. His first duty was always to his wife – his wrist tattooed with 'True love Nancy' – so he went back to Weatherhead's. His selfless example would weigh heavily on the consciences of his children when it came to their own anchors holding 'in the storms of [marital] life'.

Boatbuilding was second best for Dick Bellany but it did not diminish the pride he took in his new

Dick Bellany, 1964

John Bellany's grandparents,
1964

work or the pride his family felt for him. The launching of a new boat was always a great occasion in Port Seton or Eyemouth. A family photograph records the launch of the *Scheherazade* one snowy day in the mid-1950s. It was a special event because she was a luxury yacht, showing that the orders were by no means all local or to do with the fishing industry.

John's biggest excitement at this time was to lay a penny piece on the railway line behind Port Seton in the hope that it would be bent by the world-famous *Flying Scotsman*. He had played around on the boats from the age of five but his first trip to the real fishing grounds, on the *Bethel*, was not until he was thirteen and then only as an onlooker.

'It was totally different to what I'd dreamed. For one thing I had no idea the seagulls would be so gigantic. When they spread their wings they're almost the size of a man, and when the net comes in they're right on top of you, making this deafening noise. I was petrified at first but you get used to it. And then, of course, when it gets stormy you never imagine just how rough it can be. You really are thrown all over the place like a matchbox. But it's liberating to be part of that elemental thing at that age, when your imagination is so fertile; and I would link it with the hymns in church – "Eternal father strong to save". Governing all your thoughts were the three big questions: "Who are we? Whence do we come? Whither do we go?" and I think that's infiltrated the work right through to the present day. By then I was also reading Scott and Stevenson, with their references to everything around me. If I'd been reading about something that happened in the American South it wouldn't have mattered, but this was actually on my doorstep. The seeds were already sown to be harvested in later years.'

In art he was beginning to make his mark, winning all the prizes at school and successfully casting his net wider; his biggest triumph was to come first in a United Kingdom children's competition sponsored by Brooke Bond and BBC Television. There are fine examples of his work from this period: a drawing of the carcase of a boat – a wreck which can still be seen on the southern coast of the Forth – its robust style derived from Van Gogh, his admiration for whom had been kindled by seeing Kirk Douglas in *Lust for Life*, the film based on Van Gogh's career; and an oil painting of old Sonnie Maltman in his armchair, a portrait of technical assurance and exceptional empathy for a boy of sixteen. His Maltman grandparents lived with them in Port Seton after Sonnie retired, cementing in youth the relationship forged in infancy. Bellany was to paint his grandmother more than his parents.

On Saturdays and during school holidays he worked at Jock Dickson's gutting fish and smoking finnan haddock. It was a tough job, especially in the cold Scottish winter mornings. Both visually and spiritually this had a profound effect on his painting, and images from these formative experiences would recur again and again in his work. Once more it was a mixture of the sacred and the profane: some of the women were members of the Plymouth Brethren, the holiest of the holy, while others – especially the men – were of a more earthly disposition. The overriding ambience, though, was one of fun and affection. From these poignant experiences many of his major works have evolved.

Snapshots of the time show a good-looking boy turning into a handsome man; from the scowling 'Courtier' at the side of the Gala Queen, which made the front page of the *Sunday Post*, to the 'Mod' in embroidered waistcoat – 'Kirk Douglas's double', according to Alan Bold. At Preston Lodge in Prestonpans he became Secretary of the Rambling Club. His job was to write up and illustrate all the trips made by the club and he became an expert local historian. There was plenty to see and the landmarks remain a source of pride. He is still thrilled to think that the view from his boyhood window of the island of Inchkeith in the Forth was the same that inspired Stevenson to write *Treasure Island*; that the ruin of Fast Castle was the home of Scott's *Bride of Lammermoor*; and that in the hinterland lie the bare, bleak Lammermuirs themselves, still a heather wilderness for all the world's changes.

John Bellany, 1952

'We used to cycle and walk all over the Borders – to Melrose Abbey, Dryburgh, the Walter Scott country. I remember doing a drawing of Tantallon Castle with the Bass Rock in the distance.'

Port Seton had its own sights and legends: the reversed cup in its saucer surmounting the Garleton Monument; the whale's jawbone on the summit of Berwick Law; several associations with Mary, Queen of Scots. It was her first port of call when she arrived from France. Golf Drive, where the Bellanys had their house, recalled her introduction to the national game; and the village's signature tune was *The Four Maries*:

> *Yestre'en the Queen had four Maries*
> *The nicht she'll ha'e but three*
> *There was Mary Seton and Mary Beaton*
> *and Mary Carmichael and me*

'There was plenty to tickle the imagination', and plenty has found its way into his imagery, most insistently the Bass Rock – 'the biggest rock in the world' – three miles off the coast to the south; and Fidra lighthouse, symbol of hope and fruition.

There had always been a piano in the house, not such a rare item of furniture in the days before the domination of television, and his mother played; from the age of eight John had lessons. He also learned the accordion. Both skills have proved great social assets. He never used to give a lecture without finishing with a tune, most memorably at the National Galleries of Australia. But he has given up performing since he stopped drinking, the two having gone hand-in-hand. In Port Seton it led to 'the cultural sensation of East Lothian, "the Blue Bonnets Dance Band"!' with Shug Martin on the drums and skulls, Charlie Valentine and Bill Waters on accordion and 'yours truly tickling the ivories'.

It was of a piece with the general camaraderie: 'Nowadays people'll go in and out of Edinburgh by car but then we'd go by bus, and not like a London bus, where nobody speaks to each other, but with

Detail from *Portrait of Helen*, 1964

The Blue Bonnets, 1963, with John Bellany playing the piano

everybody yap-yap-yapping their heads off because everybody knew each other. So, between the cigarette smoke, the whisky and the beer fumes, the people laughing and joking – there was always a sign saying "Spitting Prohibited"! – it was quite a party. There was often fighting, too. If you came on after nine at night you could be pretty certain of a skirmish. And there was plenty of singing.'

Another highlight was the boat trip undertaken by Port Seton Hibs Supporters Club when Hibernian were playing away to East Fife. Bellany had connections with the team. Married to John's half-cousin was Willie Ormond, the Scottish international and member of Hibs' legendary 'Famous Five', who, as manager of Scotland, led the national side to the great unbeaten run in the 1974 World Cup; and John Dickson, skipper of the *Sunshine* and one of the directors of the club, was the father of a boy in John's class.

'The *Sunshine* would be decked out with flags and all the Port Seton football supporters would climb aboard and off we'd sail the fourteen miles across the Firth of Forth. There would be lots of Highland nectar and beer for the trip so the homeward voyage – especially if we'd won – would be pretty boisterous with much singing and celebration. Images of these experiences have crept into my more recent painting.'

Life with the Blue Bonnets prepared him for most social situations he was to encounter: 'It wasn't like the art school skirmishes, this was real fighting; especially at the Miners Welfare Clubs at Macmerry and Prestonpans or Friday night at The Johnny Cope. You had to do quite a bit of ducking behind the piano on the occasional night when the bottles were flying, but that was all part of the fun. As long as the band kept playing there was a semblance of law and order. Sometimes the most violent things were the weddings. It would start so sedately with the bridal waltz, but by about 10.30 there would be a couple of wee skirmishes and by midnight all hell had broken loose. The cause of the trouble was usually religious, between the Orangemen and the Catholic factions. But there was always plenty of high spirits and high jinks.'

It was now Bellany first got a taste for the 'amber nectar', as he puts it, and found the appeal of Jasper's pub proving stronger than that of the kirk. The band were much in demand at local dances and other functions in the neighbourhood, part of a rural way of life that has been practised for centuries and which would have been entirely familiar to Robert Burns or David Wilkie. In the 1960s it was more rustic than today, with the additional encouragement of the folksong revival, but it still goes on, despite the pervasive influence of the disco.

The Blue Bonnets monopolised Bellany's weekends almost to the end of his Edinburgh Art College days. Sandy Moffat sometimes stood in on double bass, and after Bellany began courting Helen Percy she would join in the singing or on the maracas, 'but not the dancing; John would have none of that'. Their love affair introduced yet more painful moral duplicity. Weekends with Bellany's parents in Port Seton would necessitate sabbath visits to the kirk where as likely as not there would be a hell-fire sermon on the dire consequences of the sins of the flesh.

The wall mural in Rose Street South Lane, Edinburgh

Edinburgh Festival Exhibition on the railings outside the Royal Scottish Academy, 1965

CHAPTER 3

Up Anchor

With Sandy Moffat, 1963

John Bellany was the first boy from Port Seton to go to Edinburgh College of Art, which he entered 'as a young hopeful' in October 1960. William Gillies was the principal and Robin Philipson head of painting. The Scottish curriculum required students to start with a two-year general course. Bellany intensely disliked some aspects of this, especially basic design, but considers it greatly superior to the present arrangement, which is both slapdash and narrow, with students being taught a different subject every week.

It was hard work. Classes began at 9 a.m. and continued until 9 p.m., if the voluntary evening life class was attended. The only compulsory drawing was of drapery and antique casts. Life drawing was not on the curriculum until the third year, so Bellany attended evening classes in it which were open to anyone. Members of the public had to pay, but for full-time students it was free. Additional drawing of the female nude after 6 p.m. tended to take place in other venues as part of 'field activities', as the artist politely puts it.

The controlled structure of the official course and Bellany's impatience to be an artist made him a troublesome student.

'For basic design the teachers would set these projects; and they would say something like: "The project this week is for a logo." And people would do Jaguar cars, all neatly presented and mounted. But I didn't know what a "logo" was. And they'd come round to me and say: "What've you got?" And I'd have done something like finnan haddock cutlets! I had so many rows with Kingsley Cook, who was head of design; but the biggest confrontation arose at the end of the first year when we had to pass an exam and were asked to do a record cover. I thought: "I'd better try my hardest and do a really good job with this record cover otherwise they'll fail me." So I did a really rip-roaring Jackson Pollock kind of thing – with dripped gloss paint, collaged tin-tops, really jazzy – and called it something like "Thelonius Monk at Prestonpans Town Hall". It was really poshly done, letraset, beautifully wrapped; but, the next thing, one of the examiners, Bob Callender, who taught painting and design, came along and said: "I think you've overstepped the mark this time. You're in big trouble." And I said: "I can't understand this, I really tried my best! There must be folk worse than me." So I went and saw Kingsley Cook in his office and he was purple with rage. "What have I done wrong?" I said. "Don't make it worse, just shut your mouth! You were asked to design a record cover. This design of yours is *rectangular*!" And I hadn't done it intentionally at all! I was so keen I'd just forgotten all about a record cover being square. But I got off with some holiday chore through the summer.'

Sandy Moffat, who joined the college at the same time and remains his closest friend, remembers Bellany's disagreements with the design department centring on the complaint that the presentation of his work was not neat enough. For the department presentation was crucial, but for John art was all. 'If you got a Rembrandt drawing you could nail it on a lavatory door and it would still be a great drawing!' he exclaimed in exasperation to the assembled staff.

Just what was meant by 'art' was another matter. For Bellany and Moffat in their first term it was impressionism, the style also favoured by their teachers. The college was a backwater, resisting change and deploring debates which were already being aired in the popular press. As early as 1956 the artist John Minton was quoted in the *Daily Express* saying: 'Painting is outdated, like the horse and the cart. Modern art is going nowhere. Traditional art – it's all been done before. The cinema, the theatre, possibly television, are the mediums [sic] in which painters must express themselves.'[9]

Minton's outburst was encouraged by his dislike, as a figurative painter, of the new fashion for abstract painting in Paris and, more threateningly, New York. The only Scottish abstract painter of international note was the COBRA artist William Gear, whose prize-winning abstraction at the 1951 Festival of Britain had caused a public outcry in the press and hostile questions in the House of Commons. But Gear, a former student of Edinburgh College of Art, had long since left Scotland and, in common with all his exiled countrymen, his birthright was no longer acknowledged. The ferociously expressive style of painting practised by Alan Davie, another former student, was also strongly disapproved of by the staff. 'Gillies thought anyone crossing Hadrian's Wall was out of order, unless it was him, of course,' says Bellany.

At Preston Lodge Bellany's art teacher, with typically severe Scottish logic, had warned him against art history as being too 'opinionated'. He advised him to read the history of architecture but nonetheless, did encourage his drawing and painting. He later became a good friend of Bellany. This attitude also prevailed in private education. At Sandy Moffat's public school, Daniel Stewart's, the College of Art was an option – unlike at Preston Lodge – but only for the study of architecture; painting was a hobby, to be indulged in at weekends. This remains the accepted view in Britain, despite the increase in public awareness of the visual arts over the last thirty years.

Art history at the college was taught by T. Elder Dickson, nicknamed 'The Dome': 'dry as a stick, spouting Berenson way over our heads'. Bellany does not recall a teacher citing a poet or novelist throughout his time at college. Gillies, in particular, was notoriously anti-intellectual. His policy was to teach skills and let ideas look after themselves. This did not satisfy Bellany, whose yearning for intellectual challenge was now met by his friendship with Sandy Moffat and Alan Bold.

Moffat and Bold were members of a modern jazz quartet but it was more than a shared ability to play music that brought Bellany, Bold and Moffat together. As Bold has written: 'We tended to look at the world as a territory divided between Them and Us. To Them we gladly conceded the concept of life as a long process of building a career and accumulating possessions. As for Us, we were wholly involved in an exploration of aesthetic matters. John Bellany was definitely one of Us.'[10] It was a powerful, mutually beneficial combination of personalities and experience. Bellany's naïve exuberance and single-minded determination to be a painter was matched by the others' greater sophistication, intellectual breadth and, in the case of the Marxist Alan Bold, political radicalism.

It was the beatnik era and symptomatic that their first historic meeting took place in a bar. Their discussions would rarely be unaccompanied by a drink. 'I discovered it wasn't just the Blue Bonnets Dance Band that was keen on the Highland nectar and the thirst,' recalls Bellany. 'These guys in Edinburgh were quite expert at it as well. The *joie de vivre* made you want to be the most outrageous student in the world, not just a quiet wee schoolboy; and we were ace at enjoying ourselves. The Beatles were choirboys compared with the way we behaved!'

Alan Bold was the intellectual of the trio. He was reading English Literature at Edinburgh University and was already making a name for himself as a poet. Sartre and D.H. Lawrence were the fashionable writers but it was Bold who introduced Bellany to Joyce's *Ulysses*, the imaginative freedom of which anticipated that of modern jazz. Bold and Moffat's cool quartet had their new friend changing the repertoire of the Blue Bonnets. It was not long before the Miners Welfare, who had yet to discover Louis Armstrong, were treated to Bellany's interpretation of Thelonius Monk. 'I got quite snooty about it,' he remembers.

Impressionism was soon abandoned as being too genteel for their adventurous spirits. Their new hero was Alan Davie, with whose rejection of Scottish parochialism they warmly identified. He was an intoxicatingly free and romantic spirit: a glider pilot, stream-of-consciousness jazz saxophonist and painter, whose dislike of academic orthodoxy was a point of honour. As the poet Michael Horovitz noted in his book on the artist in 1963: 'Revisiting art schools to teach, Davie recalls his horror of the life class

– its mechanical pursuit of photographic proportions, surface exactitude and illusionistic perspective. His accomplished skirmishes with such concepts doubtless intensified the expressive freshness of true "life" drawing when he came to it – often by means of "bad" drawing and composition, allowing distortions their rightful place.'[11]

In their free time Bellany and Moffat began to paint, like Davie before them, in the freely expressive style of Jackson Pollock, the fire of their enthusiasm fanned by the hostility of the college staff: 'We became "the wild men of Borneo" before the end of our first term.'

Boozing was very much part of this 'macho' artistic image. John commuted to the college by bus from Port Seton but this did not prevent him getting to know the Rose Street bars. The normal progress of his pub crawls with Bold and Moffat was from Paddy's to The Abbotsford and finally to Milne's. Paddy's took its name from the owner, Paddy Crossan, and included some notable members of the Edinburgh intelligentsia among its regulars. The most interesting were Sydney Goodsir Smith, poet and art critic for *The Scotsman*; John Tonge, an expert on the work of the elder McTaggart, who had known Sickert and been a crony of the inseparable Scottish painters Colquhoun and MacBryde; the Orcadian writer George Mackay Brown; and the poet Robert Garioch. All were convivial drinking companions and, considering the difference in age, remarkably generous in their acceptance of the young. Garioch, in particular, was a teasing fount of uproarious laughter; and Goodsir Smith an active promoter who reviewed their first public shows.[12] Paddy Crossan, too, actively encouraged Bellany's talent, commissioning him to do a mural of Rose Street behind the lobster bar and buying a painting of the blind accordionist who played at the door, which he hung over the fireplace. These no longer exist but a surprising scatter of antique casts still decorate one wall. They were saved by Paddy when they were thrown out by the college in a fit of reforming zeal in the late 1960s. Bellany has a painting of these casts, a robust tribute to his competence, done in 1961 when they were still a prescribed part of the curriculum.

The Abbotsford provided Rose Street's biggest social melting-pot. Bank managers and company directors would 'souk' at the bar alongside the workmen who had humped the barrels of beer into the basement. One evening during the Edinburgh Festival, Bellany had a drink with the conductor Giulini, then at the height of his fame. Milne's Bar, with its maze of basement rooms, was the wildest and most wanton.

It was typical of Bellany's exuberance that Helen Percy's first memory of him is hammering out jazz on the piano with a fishing net over his head. This was at a Freshers' concert in 1961, the start of his second year. She was in her first year and came from Golspie in the north of Scotland. She kept an eye out for him from then on, impressed by his wild and rebellious presence and by the power of his paintings.

Bellany decided to move out of his parents' house and stay in Edinburgh for his second year. He lived for a while in the Dean Village but then, with Moffat and two other students, rented what they called 'the studio', a top-floor flat at 150 Rose Street Lane South, behind the west end of Princes Street. In 1994 the numerals he painted in immaculate italics thirty years before still survived by the main door.

The rent was £1 a week and among the tenants was a snooping meths drinker who, Bellany says, had the reddest-rimmed eyes he has ever seen. The studio consisted of four small rooms with coom ceilings and a toilet with cold-running tap. There was no kitchen. There was, however, one windfall: in an old ottoman they discovered a fine collection of nineteenth-century engravings of the Old Masters. Bellany covered the walls with them and studied them throughout his student days, donating most of them to the college when he graduated.

Outside the Tate Gallery, London, with Sandy Moffat and Alan Bold, after viewing the Kokoschka exhibition, 1961

Sandy Moffat, John Bellany, Alan Bold and Hugh MacDiarmid, Milne's Bar, Edinburgh, 1964

CHAPTER 4

The Turn of the Tide

The summer of 1962 marked a turning point. Troublesome students are the best and this was acknowledged when Bellany and Moffat were awarded two-year Andrew Grant travel scholarships. In college they had followed the curriculum; but in the Rose Street studio they had been painting in an abstract-expressionist style. Prompted by Bold's Marxist call for a socialist art they began to question whether 'modern' necessarily meant 'abstract'.

'By this time people like Ad Rheinhardt were coming on the scene saying "painting's dead"; so we had a philosophical rethink and decided that if painting was the great thing we thought it was we'd have to start from scratch. We studied the wonderful collection of photogravure reproductions we'd discovered and thought: "What's the drip and dribble compared with this? These things are timeless; they're great." I suppose it was just growing up. We were no longer content with light entertainment, Radio 2. We'd graduated to maybe Radio 4, not Radio 3 yet, but certainly we were setting ourselves harder tasks and being more self-critical.'[13]

In this spirit Bold, Bellany and Moffat travelled to London for the first time to see exhibitions by Alan Davie and Oscar Kokoschka. After touring Soho they settled down for the night on some benches in Trafalgar Square. A policeman soon appeared and told them to move on, but it turned out he was from Tranent so they were given star treatment and allowed to sleep where they liked. Next day they toured the shows. Davie retained their respect but it was Kokoschka who pointed the way forward to a renewed humanism.

Bellany abandoned his fashionable flirtation with international abstraction to paint about Scotland from his own experience. With this in mind, he and Moffat studied the art of the past and the figurative masters of the twentieth century, consciously allying themselves with a northern tradition of Breughel, Bosch, Cranach, Grunewald, Rembrandt and Goya, an 'honorary' northerner, whose scorn of hypocrisy Bellany compared in an essay with that of Robert Burns.

He now began to visit the National Gallery[14] and the National Gallery of Modern Art at Inverleith

House in the Royal Botanic Gardens, newly opened with Douglas Hall as keeper.[15] Hall's internationalism and his bias towards European as opposed to the more fashionable American art set an inspiring example. 'To the detriment of my standing in the profession I was uninterested in the dominant class of contemporary artists who adopted a knowing sort of progressivism as the badge of their clan,' he has subsequently written.[16] One of the first of Hall's many far-sighted purchases for the permanent collection of the new gallery was a painting by the COBRA artist Karel Appel, *Dance in Space before the Storm.* Bellany's favourite twentieth-century artists were now Fernand Léger, whose 1950 oil on canvas study for *The Builders* (*Les Constructeurs*) at the new National Gallery of Modern Art he particularly admired, and Picasso – 'Mr P, the king of them all'.

The appeal of Léger lay in his socialism as well as his art, a political awareness encouraged by Alan Bold's radicalism. Bold was now editor of *Gambit*, the university's literary magazine, and it was through him that Bellany read – and, in August 1962, met – Hugh MacDiarmid. For Bellany, 'to read Joyce was one thing but actually to find a living giant just as big and to get to talk to him, that was quite another'.

MacDiarmid was in his sixties and had been sidelined as a crank by the anglicised Scottish establishment, thanks largely to his Stalinist communism – he had been one of the few western intellectuals to support the invasion of Hungary in 1956 – and passionate advocacy of Scottish independence. He had been a founder member of the Scottish National Party, but in practical terms he was a romantic idealist, an anarchist at heart. 'He was a bit of a swot, an aloof man. He lived in a cottage at Biggar and only came into Edinburgh once a month, though from the history books you'd think he'd been in Milne's Bar all the time. He was a great lecturer, fiery, but he should really have been head of studies at the university. He wasn't a one-to-one man in the pub, like Sydney Goodsir Smith. He might let you tug the hem of his garment once in a while, but that was all. He was an élitist; a platform man.'

This did not prevent him being a great poet, which he was and said he was. MacDiarmid's poetry and invective, with its call for a truly Scottish art, true to specific experience and language precisely to break the bounds of parochialism, made the profoundest impression. As he wrote in his 'Third Hymn to Lenin':

> *For I am not an Englishman, but utterly different,*
> *And I throw Scotland's challenge at the English again;*
> *Mine is the antipathy of the internationalist to the nationalist,*
> *The cosmopolitan to the Englishman,*
> *The doctrinate to the opportunist,*
> *The potential fanatic to the 'practical man'.*[17]

How could any young Scot with the fire of Wallace in his belly resist?

'I've been working my way through "A Drunk Man Looks at the Thistle" again,' Bellany wrote to Moffat in 1962, 'and it is much better with a second reading and no doubt better still at the one-hundred-and-second reading. We're really fortunate in having MacDiarmid as an example.'

MacDiarmid's poetry was far in advance of anything in Scottish painting. Internationally recognised as a writer of world stature, he had written poetry on universal themes in the Scottish vernacular, whereas the painters seemed content to have no higher aim than to decorate the sitting-rooms of the well-off with bland landscapes and still-lifes. They had no ambition to change the world or even to upset convention. It was in reaction to this that Bellany began to paint in a Scottish accent of his own, in a spirit of Christian socialism. 'I don't think he's ever been very political,' confirms Alan Bold. 'I think he detests the idea of party politics, really. He has led his life in terms of heroic figures and all his heroes are artists.'

That first term of his third year he finally met Helen when he introduced himself at an evening life-drawing class. He complimented her on her drawing and she was struck by his gentleness. 'I thought, "This is amazing. There's a completely different side to him." There was none of the aggressive, brash façade.' By that Christmas she had moved into the flat.

'Whatever you do, don't come home with a fellow with long hair and a beard,' Helen's parents had told her before she left home for the college. Bellany prudently had it cut before visiting them for the first time in the new year, but not short enough. There was considerable disapproval in Golspie and rumour ran riot that he was a member of a weird religious sect. Helen was struck by John's mature acceptance of the situation. He explained to her that it was simply because they were not used to it, as that particular 1960s' fashion had not reached Sutherland. However, Bellany and Harold Percy, Helen's father, hit it off, having the same roguish sense of humour and talent for performing; and in due course John became a great favourite in the village. His credentials as the son of fishing people was a further recommendation since Helen's mother's family came from a fishing background – her grandfather had been a fish curer and several of her relatives had boats.

In April 1963 Bellany, Moffat and Bold took advantage of the Andrew Grant travel scholarships they had won to visit Paris for the first time. 'Official documents' from the art college, which might have helped them, proved useless, but from their base in the Quartier Latin, the dilapidated Nouvel Hotel, they managed to complete a survey of French painting since the Revolution.

Considering the importance of the skate in Bellany's art, that strange fish which has a 'face' and is unique in also having external sexual organs – the cause of many fishy stories – it is not surprising that to see Chardin's *La Raie* was a striking moment of confirmation. But it was the works of the Romantics which fired his ambition, particularly the massive masterpieces of David, Ingres, Géricault, Delacroix and Courbet in the gallery of nineteenth-century paintings at the Louvre (sadly now rearranged). They made him determined to paint on an epic scale. 'It would be impossible to exaggerate the impact these great "machines" had on John,' Moffat wrote in 1986.[18]

The effect soon found expression. The nearest backyard from the Rose Street flat belonged to a Greek restaurant but was never used; so, with some assistance from Helen, Bellany made a mural incorporating a real, semi-exposed piano. Boldly-outlined portraits of Helen and John in the manner of Léger covered the stones on either side with the daubed piano in the middle. No permission was sought, but when the restaurant's owners found out they took it in good part, encouraging their clientele to have a look. The restaurant and piano are now long gone, but flecks of paint still mark the stones.

The piano was a protest against the restrictions of college life and the prim requirements of bourgeois taste. Music spoke to all, so why not art? And it also had a socialist intent by taking art out of the exclusive domain of the galleries. Bold's radicalism no doubt spurred Bellany and Moffat to take a more political stance. Bold now had his own Marxist publication, the *Rocket*, to which they contributed, and he had introduced them to the art criticism of the Marxist John Berger, especially as promulgated in his book *Permanent Red*. 'Berger wrote simply, no grey areas,' says Bold, 'which John liked.' The Marxist Ernst Fischer's *Necessity of Art* was another of Bellany's favourites. He tended to do his reading in the George IV Bridge Library, finding the college's facilities inadequate for his growing requirements.

The socialist Courbet was the most exemplary artistic influence; not only had he painted everyday scenes of rural life from his own experience on a scale previously reserved for noble subjects, but he had been the first artist to propose an alternative to the Academy. It was in emulation of this, and to take the Rose Street painting one stage further, that Bellany and Moffat decided to hold an exhibition of their work on the railings of Castle Terrace during the Edinburgh Festival in August 1963.

Bellany's largest pictures, in the style and festive colours of Fernand Léger, were on ten-by-eight-feet hardboard. 'When you're young and learning, you have to have periods when you're overinfluenced, as happened to me when I had a little six-month affair with Léger. But through that I learned an enormous amount about composition and I saw the link between Léger and Poussin.'

The weather was dry and the park's bushes and flowers formed a complementary background. Nothing sold but the work was seen by thousands of passers-by. He also learned the invaluable lesson that knowledge comes from action. Some of the exhibits were transcriptions, one of them of Giorgione's *Peccam Petra*, which, says Bellany, 'forced me to confront and solve problems of composition on a grand scale, of which I would have had no inkling if I'd been less foolhardy'.

The new term saw his appointment as president of the students sketch club and in that position he argued for a more outward-looking attitude among the students, urging them to submit their paintings for that year's 'Young Contemporaries' exhibition in London. 'I was becoming quite an evangelist, spreading the gospel, so I took it all on myself. "Just put your paintings in the sculpture yard and I'll see to it," I said, not really having a clue how we were going to pay to transport them to London. In the end there were about fifty paintings. There was never going to be any money, so we had to be a bit dare-devil and smuggle them down south. I used to work on the Christmas mail at Waverley Station and I made this plan that we'd whip them into the guard's van on the 8.20 evening train, which was quiet, the mail train really, with not many passengers around. Bill Gillon and I would be the ones to travel.

'We took the paintings along in a rickety van, nice and early, and put them in the left luggage. Then we hung around until five to eight when we got this big bogey, carted them along to the guard's van and started loading up as quick as we could. The guys at the station all knew me so that was okay, but halfway through the guard appeared. "What the hell are you up to?" he demanded. We'd already got twenty-five paintings in the van, most of them whopping eight-by-sixers, with the other half still to go. "It's our luggage", I said. "Well, you're staying right where you are, young man. Get the police," he called to one of the staff. Next minute the police arrived and while they were questioning us the train pulled out with half the paintings still on board. Next the stationmaster appeared, in top hat and tails in those days, and we were frog-marched to his office with what felt like half of Edinburgh having a gloat. The stationmaster asked who we were responsible to so we grudgingly said Robin Philipson, thinking this was definitely the end of our student careers. Philipson soon appeared, all decked out for some posh dinner. But instead of going at us, he went for them. It was brilliant: "How dare you treat my students in this way? Don't you realise these are valuable works of art you've got on your train! I want the whole matter dealt with immediately."'

Philipson's magisterial intervention saved their skins and also ensured a safe passage for the paintings. After it was over he took them to the station buffet, gave them a drink and left them with a fiver for expenses in London. As Carel Weight, later Bellany's professor at the Royal College of Art, has said with regard to John's time at Edinburgh: 'The keystone was Robin Philipson who really loved him and admired his work greatly. He talked a lot about him.'

The trouble was worth it. Bellany and Moffat were both accepted for the exhibition, the first time young Scottish painters had made the cut for the 'Young Contemporaries'. They subsequently became regular contributors to this prestigious event. Bellany's entry was *Mon Hélène à Moi*, six by eight feet on hardboard, a painting owing much to Modigliani and Léger. 'It's a complicated painting for a third-year student. I felt I was getting somewhere for the first time.'

Bursting with new confidence Bellany and Moffat proceeded to revolutionise the life class, which as third-year students they were now entitled to attend. They discovered a cupboard full of sumptuous drapes which they brought into the life room, and encouraged the models to adopt more abandoned poses. Instead of little easel paintings they attempted life-size depictions on hardboard.

For the 'revel' or Christmas party, when the students were allowed to decorate the college as they pleased, Bellany wangled a free load of cardboard from a local factory and painted some vast works to fill the ninety-foot-long walls. It marked a breakthrough in scale for him.

The notoriety of the Castle Terrace exhibition made them realise they had created a polemical situation, which they determined to exploit. Acting in concert with Alan Bold, who wrote tracts in support of their anti-establishment intentions, they had the audacity in 1964 and 1965 to win a street-trader's licence from the City Council to show their work on the Mound, the site of the Royal Scottish Academy and the National Gallery of Scotland. For a minimal sum they were allowed to use the railings flanking the garden side of the RSA and the National Gallery throughout the three weeks of the Festival. Every visitor to Edinburgh was virtually certain to see their work; added to which there was the free publicity of a pipe band, which played behind their patch every morning at eleven. Considering the difficulties young painters always face when trying to exhibit their work, it was a wonderfully bold stroke and one that has deservedly entered folk legend.

The paintings, all on massive pieces of hardboard, were stored each night at Milne's Bar in Hanover Street, courtesy of Bob Watt, the landlord; nevertheless the journey to and fro was a back-breaking business – like plying their way through a rough sea, especially if Edinburgh's notorious winds were blowing. Bellany took the public tour of *The Raft of the Medusa* as their precedent, mistakenly assuming in his youthful enthusiasm that the consumptive Géricault had personally humped his vast canvas round the church halls of Scotland. This romantic simplification – the painting was publicly shown but only in London and Dublin and by an entrepreneur, not the artist – served its purpose, as the thought of it lightened their daily load.

Bellany's paintings for the first time depicted the life of Port Seton, which was now for him what the village of Ornans had been to Courbet. The most famous of these paintings, today in the collection

Fishermen in the Snow, exhibited on the railings, Edinburgh Festival, 1965. The painting now hangs in the Ministry of Agriculture and Fisheries Building, Edinburgh

With Sandy Moffat outside the Royal Scottish Academy, 1964

of the Scottish National Gallery of Modern Art, is *Allegory* (1964), a huge triptych in oil on hardboard dominated by the cornucopian forms of three gutted and staked haddock, with a miniaturised crowd of fishing folk in the background. The idea was born when Bellany was struck by the cruciform appearance of haddock pinned up to dry when he was working as a fish-gutter; and a preparatory sketch shows that he intended to set the scene inside a fish-gutting shed. The immemorial fish-symbol of Christ had long been familiar to him, but by 1964 wider artistic influences had come to bear. The meticulous style is Rembrandt-esque, the mood Breughelian and the most specific reference is to Bacon's *Painting* (1946), now in the Museum of Modern Art, New York, which shows a figure seated at a table beneath a side of beef. But this is an unmistakable Bellany. In an otherwise critical review in 1989 Brian Sewell wrote: 'The painting is a host of references to established painters, but obeisant to none of them – it is a visionary recognition of the cruelty and suffering inflicted by ordinary men in the pursuits of daily life, an acknowledgment of the inevitable cycle of death and survival.'[19]

Allegory was not bought, unsurprising considering its uncompromising size, but Bellany did pick up a commission from the Ministry of Agriculture and Fisheries to paint some murals for Chesser House, Edinburgh (the result, *Fishers in the Snow*, is still there); and the award of a post-graduate scholarship allowed Bellany and Moffat to repeat the experiment in 1965. They saw to it that the publicity increased every year ('we weren't twits') to include reports or reviews in all the leading Scottish newspapers and even appearances on the TV news. They benefited from the lack of local competition, adding a touch of youthful spirit to the occasion. Fun they had, but not at the expense of seriousness. 'Painting's not dead while we're still alive', was their defiant slogan, challenging the attitudes even of the international avant-garde as it progressed towards what Bellany dismissed as 'Invisibilism', or abstraction pursued to its absurd and minimal conclusion. But there was what he later recognised as 'an obverse side to the coin'.

In their devotion to realism they were blind to the merit of Matisse, whom they despised as the main influence on what they called the 'pasticheurs' of the Royal Scottish Academy. It was typical of their attitude that one of the few Scottish paintings they admired was James Guthrie's bleak 1882 tribute to Courbet, *A Highland Funeral* (Glasgow Museums and Art Galleries). It was not until after his transplant operation twenty-five years later that Bellany would write to Moffat, in capital letters: 'COLOUR IS THE MOST IMPORTANT THING'.

That September John and Helen were married in a typically riotous Highland wedding at St Andrew's Church, Golspie. They spent their honeymoon in Dieppe, because of its artistic associations with Sickert, Braque and many others. As a result it is a town of great significance to them, enforced by the liver failure Bellany suffered there on a family outing in 1984.

Carel Weight was an external assessor at various Scottish art colleges, including Edinburgh, and Philipson had drawn his attention to Bellany. Weight considered the Port Seton works 'extraordinary, sincere statements', finding him personally 'a larger-than-life character, a young man of immense promise', and suggested he should prolong his post-graduateship by coming to the Royal College of Art. Edinburgh is a notoriously narrow art college. A large percentage of its students are born locally and almost its entire staff are former pupils, the same applying today just as much as thirty years ago. True to this tradition Gillies flatly refused to lend the college's support to the application, on the grounds that Bellany knew all he needed to know; but John went ahead independently. He applied to the college and was duly accepted as a candidate for the week-long entrance exam in London in the summer of 1965. 'There was never any doubt he would pass it,' says Weight, but Helen remembers it as a nail-biting ordeal, comparable to the tests he had to take at Addenbrooke's Hospital in 1988 to see if he was capable of undergoing transplant surgery.

As a parting gesture from Edinburgh he was awarded a major travelling scholarship, which he spent with Helen in the Low Countries, not 'to produce two or three pretty Dutch landscapes or drawings of broken-down castles, but to view the work of GREAT MASTERS,' as he explained in a letter to Moffat. In fact, he did enough work *in situ* to earn him an exhibition at Dromidaris Gallery, Enkhausen, during his stay in Holland, his first in a commercial gallery. But it was seeing Breughel, Rembrandt, Van Gogh and the other Flemish and Dutch masters which made the trip so memorable.

'Things were sellotaping together in ways I wouldn't have thought possible. The faith in the northern European tradition wasn't words, wasn't theory, it was actually real. It linked with the best Scottish art. Wilkie's *Pitlessie Fair* might have been by Jan Steen. So I found we weren't out on a limb after all. What had Pop Art to do with us? There are hardly any billboards in Scotland! What had blank canvases got to do with us? So we stuck to our guns and the culture we had come from; and that included the literature, of course.'

Helen and John Bellany's first wedding, St Andrews Church, Golspie, Sutherland, September 1964

Pourquoi?, 1967, oil on board, 152.5 × 122CM, 60 × 48IN.

My Father, 1966, oil on board, 122 × 91.5CM, 48 × 36IN.
(The Scottish National Gallery of Modern Art)

Kinlochbervie, 1966, oil on board, 243.5 × 320CM. (Collection Scottish National Gallery of Modern Art)

The Fishers (The Big Haul), 1966, oil on board, 183.2 × 213.4CM, 72 × 84IN.
(Glasgow Museums: Art Gallery and Museum, Kelvingrove)

Fishers in the Snow, 1966, oil on board, 243.5 × 320CM, 96 × 126IN.

CHAPTER 5

Gathering Storm

Bellany arrived at the Royal College 'hungry for knowledge' and with Helen seven months pregnant. They had travelled south without a care – a suitcase each for their clothes, Bellany's painting gear and, his proudest possession, the model boat his father had made of *Girl Margaret*, LH 52. As soon as the boat was installed he felt at home. This has always been the case, from bedsit days to present luxury.

The bursary made no provision for marriage. For the first week they stayed in a miserable room in Earls Court. 'The big adventure starts here!' Bellany had said, flinging open the window; the view was of a funeral parlour with an acre of hearses. Next they moved to a flat in a house in Putney owned by an old Polish couple and full of equally ancient tenants. 'No pets or children' were the only conditions, so Helen disguised her pregnancy by wearing a cloak for the interview. It worked, though Bellany's conscience got the better of him as they sipped a conclusive sherry and he blurted out the truth. 'Do you think I do not notice!' exclaimed the old landlady and, turning to Helen, she said sweetly, 'You can breathe out now, dear.'

'Our situation was so precarious, it was a great relief when the kindly old couple allowed us to stay until Jonathan's birth,' he remembers. Once installed Bellany even managed secretly to do some work, painstakingly avoiding spattering any paint.

The anonymity of London, the 'lost souls' and loneliness, the joyless crowds on the tube, the lack of camaraderie after the smaller, friendlier world of Edinburgh were alienating. In his first weeks there he painted *The Escalator* and *The Missile* (now destroyed), both showing the tensions and anxieties of metropolitan life.

He was the first Scottish student to be accepted by the Royal College for fourteen years and his Lothian burr and, in the painter Peter de Francia's memory, 'rather old-fashioned ginger tweed suit', emphasised the fact. De Francia, who was then a lecturer in art history at the college, recalls that MacDiarmid was the major influence: 'He was fiercely anti the Edinburgh establishment and very keen to make his mark in London. One of them, I think Moffat, once appeared wearing a sock with a suspicious lump in it. "It's probably a dirk," said John Berger.'

The adjustment for Bellany was not easy. 'I had to take quite a lot of stick in my first year. I was treated as if the heather was coming out of my ears; but I could cope with that because of my faith in my ability. I wasn't going to be put off by some dedicated followers of fashion' – or DFFs, as he scornfully referred to them. The teaching he enjoyed: 'Each week I learned something; it was a great source of knowledge', and he enjoyed the set subject in the general studies course, social anthropology.

The cultural opportunities of London were legion after the limitations of Scotland, his excitement preserved in a lively correspondence with Sandy Moffat. He had virtually no money – as a grateful acknowledgment of a loan of £2 shows – but managed to see a wealth of exhibitions, films and plays. William Roberts's retrospective at the Tate inspired his greatest enthusiasm. He commended him to Moffat for his 'down-to-earth subjects of working-class people', noted the influence of Léger and Breughel with the eye of a fellow enthusiast, but lamented 'the loss of bite' in the later work; nonetheless he was 'one of the best English artists of his period'.

More influential was the Tate's exhibition of Max Beckmann. In the correspondence only an exclamatory 'PS Beckmann show great' registers the event. Critics have relentlessly compared Bellany with Beckmann and it is easy to see why today he is 'fed up' with the connection. His use of the triptych predates his knowledge of the older artist and is, anyway, a timeless device; and his subject matter has always been based on personal experience. Nonetheless, Beckmann's importance to him is undeniable.

Beckmann was a modern painter who had come through the fire of twentieth-century history and addressed its horrors and tragedies. In 1938 he had stated in a London lecture that 'the elimination of the human component from artistic representation is the cause of the vacuum which makes us all suffer in varying degrees . . . Human sympathy and understanding must be reinstated'.[20] In 1965 the *reductio ad absurdum* of modernist progress had not yet arrived at Bellany's 'Invisibilism' – the neon tubes of Flavin, the blank minimalist canvas – but it was under way. The central panel of Beckmann's *Departure* triptych (1932/33) (Museum of Modern Art, New York) showing a group of heraldic figures standing in a boat, had made a profound effect. It showed a way to express his own deepest conflicts and experiences in a symbolic language that was surprisingly appropriate, and he soon adopted some of its devices: the low foreground side of the boat; the standing figures; the masks; the diagonally draped net. It bound him even more securely to the Nordic tradition of a soulful, expressionist humanism. Beckmann had 'the punch' he expected of art.

The extent to which Bellany was out of step with 'swinging London', despite his long locks, was demonstrated when one of his paintings was selected for a combined exhibition of work by students at the three main London post-graduate colleges – the Royal Academy, the Slade and the Royal College. His was the only realist painting: 'It stands out like a sore thumb. I'm surrounded by aesthetic scribbles,' he reported. Matters were not improved by the blandness of the pop painter Dick Smith's 'crit' – having 'liked everything', he summed up by telling the students to make the most of the privilege of 'working alongside the best painters in the world'. 'By that do you mean the staff?' asked Bellany and brought the house down. Later he was depressed that this raucous behaviour might have offended some of his supporters. It felt like Edinburgh all over again, but his doubts proved ill-founded. The staff never wavered in their support. 'He had a lovely sense of fun,' recalls Carel Weight. 'Curiously enough there is a parallel with John Bratby. Bratby was English but he too was immensely gifted as a student. Both worked very rapidly and had enormous gifts as draughtsmen and painters. And of course they were both to face up to all sorts of difficulties.' Weight speaks with the authority of having taught them both. Bratby admired Bellany's work and they enjoyed a fitful friendship until his death in 1992.

In December, at the end-of-term tutorial, the staff were astonished at Bellany's prolific output. They 'raved on about it for two hours (everybody else got about 15 minutes). They said that I had done more work in one term than most people do in three years. The amazing thing is they don't even know the names of anybody else in my year – far less their work!!!!' he wrote. Philipson was equally impressed, especially by Bellany's ability to paint such large paintings in a space the size of a telephone kiosk. Bellany complained he had no room to do big paintings, so as a special concession an arrangement was made for him to work off-limits in the college's Cromwell Road studios. He had also used up his quota of free materials. Weight offered to bend the rules to allow him more but Bellany refused. 'I said: "I'll try to wangle something for you." But he replied: "No, you won't, Carel. If I'm foolish enough to paint on this large scale I must cope with it myself." I thought that rather wonderful. A lot of people who had his ability might have been swollen-headed – he wasn't a bit.'

The studio was so cold Bellany had to wear mittens even in the summer; but it was large, and it gave him a buzz to be working near Francis Bacon in Rowland Gardens. 'I met him several times but it was more the fact of seeing him around; catching a glimpse of the great man as I was going down to The Hoop and Toy. It was a nice feeling as you were working to think he would be picking up the brushes and putting them in the turps just the same as me a few hundred yards away. It sounds daft but other artists would understand. That's why so many congregated in the South of France round Picasso and Matisse.'

One book particularly fired his imagination, the nineteenth-century writer James Hogg's *The*

Private Memoirs and Confessions of a Justified Sinner. This strange novel of religious perversion tells the story of a boy of strict Calvinist upbringing who is persuaded by a stranger, the devil personified, to commit a series of murders on the understanding that as a member of the elect no sin can deprive him of salvation. The fact that the reader is left doubting whether the devil is real or a figment of the boy's imagination makes it all the more disturbing; electrifying for Bellany. Hogg confronted many of the dilemmas raised by his own Calvinist upbringing now that he was in the wider, less innocent, world. The descriptions reminded him of the paintings of Hieronymus Bosch and the account of schizophrenia, a precursor of *Dr Jekyll and Mr Hyde*, was of an all too Scottish cast, 'especially when Highland nectar's been taken!' as Bellany puts it.

Bellany had not heard of Hogg in Scotland, where the book went suspiciously unmentioned, but in the south he became 'a wee bit of an evangelist for him' and painted *The Ettrick Shepherd*, Hogg's better known sobriquet as a poet, in his honour.

At the end of the year Helen went north to have the baby, so that she could be near her parents. Bellany followed in time for Christmas, enjoying the solitude of some long walks on the beach at Golspie. Jonathan was born in Inverness on 22 December 1965. They later moved in with friends, Jack and Margaret Murray, at 5 Sibella Road in Clapham; but got a flat of their own near Battersea Park, a great bonus when the children were growing up, in the new year.

An impressive painting of winter cold, *Fishermen in the Snow*, was completed early in 1965. It is now owned by that noted collector of his work, the pop star David Bowie. More observed than imagined, it has a timeless air in the manner of Breughel, the grouped figures and anchored boats – one 'whale-backed' in design, a recent 'improvement' at that date – harmoniously distributed across an impressive expanse of hardboard. Parenthood was more symbolically, though no less observantly, celebrated in *The Scottish Family*, where Calvinist severity is offset by the tender portrait of Helen and the newborn, tightly hugged Jonathan.

Bellany's energy and ambition were unaffected by his new responsibility. He wrote Moffat an impassioned letter itemising the need for them to put on another railings show at the Edinburgh Festival in 1966: '(1.) The green-eyed nonentities who would immediately take over would make a mockery of what our past exhibitions stood for. (2.) After the encouragement from people like Berger and de Francia I certainly would feel a bit guilty about not having one. (3.) The opportunity of free scaffolding. (4.) The belief that we are the only two painters who don't seem to be caught up in the fashionable rat-race. (5.) Our stance against the corruption of the Academy and the commercial gallery. (6.) Our duty to follow masters like Courbet and Manet who found themselves in a similar position. (7.) The chance to have our work looked at by thousands of people (some of whom must be intelligent enough to see what we are doing). (8.) Our belief in the revitalising of a dead tradition to the world. WE MUST HAVE THAT FESTIVAL SHOW!!! It means hard work but no great master was afraid of that.' His self-confidence has a MacDiarmid ring and he was disappointed by Moffat's refusal.

As this letter proves, Peter de Francia, who had studied under Léger for four years and had known Beckmann, was the teacher whom Bellany most respected at the Royal College; and it was through de Francia that he met John Berger. De Francia and Berger both had a Marxist faith in the socialist role of art, championing figurative work. As in Edinburgh Bellany was now president of the students sketch club and invited Berger to judge its annual show. He unhesitatingly chose Bellany's *Three Fishers* as the winner. It was not a popular decision with the older students, the 'op-pop factory of DFFs', but it was thoroughly deserved. *Three Fishers* retains its power, the crudity of its construction – three large bits of hardboard tacked together – grittily in keeping with its labouring subject, a grittiness subsequently complemented by the accidental addition of some seagull droppings collected in storage in Port Seton. They even match tonally and Bellany now considers them part of the painting. De Francia still considers these early paintings of 'grim fishermen' among the most powerful of all Bellany's works, 'remarkable for a student and quite unlike anything done in Britain at the time'.

Reactionary Bellany may have been, but not parochial. 'I went to the Royal Academy – the dregs of the art world. I fainted when I saw a whole big wall entitled SCOTTISH PAINTERS and goggled at the usual derivative muck. The usual batch of Scottish paintings left me unimpressed.' As for the 'so-called Academicians' they were 'rubbish'. Even Bratby was criticised for pandering to popular taste with a picture of jingoistic bunting. As usual with Bellany it was 'NOTHINGNESS' or, another favourite insult, 'vacuity', which he deplored. By his reckoning it was a fault now endemic to abstract art.

At the end of his first academic year he was summoned before the Dean. He expected a stern warning for having bunked off tutorials but was pleasantly surprised to find himself being congratulated for scoring the highest essay mark. An invitation to the graduation dinner followed, gaining him admittance to the hallowed senior common-room, or 'staff boozer', as he preferred to call it: 'What a place – fitted carpets, big couches and a painting by each member of staff on the wall.' At the 'nosh-up', which he made the most of, 'all that was missing was a paper hat each'; but it did not prevent him noting the Breughelian qualities in a Lowry. He ended a spicy account on a homesick note: 'I really miss you all down here! Because there's really nobody I can look upon as a real friend who you can enjoy boozing with and talking to for ages. Most people down here are so wrapped up in their fashionable career-conscious world.'

With Helen and their son
Jonathan in Bellany's studio at
the Royal Academy. Behind them
is *Kinlochbervie*, which now
hangs in the Scottish National
Gallery of Modern Art

With Jonathan in front of the
Barbara Hepworth sculpture,
Battersea Park, 1966

The Bellany family, 1977

Moffat remembers him detesting ' "toffee-nosed" intellectuals and artists who talked about nothing but ART. The English art scene, he felt, was dominated by such types, or "yappers" as he preferred to call them.'[21]

'I believe's it's imperative,' Bellany wrote in another 1966 letter, 'that one is really excited and overwhelmed by the things one paints or writes about – I don't need to quote any examples to prove this.'

Moffat and Bold visited London as often as they could. Moffat recalls weekends of non-stop intellectual action: 'We would often talk until early morning, raving on with Slav-like intensity, entirely consumed by artistic matters and problems. Next day we would be raring to go again.'[22]

Such intense exchanges came to a climax in the summer of 1967 when he visited East Germany. The Scottish Composers Guild had been invited by the East German government to attend a Handel festival and when insufficient members failed to respond, Ronald Stevenson, the composer and pianist, invited Bold, Bellany and Moffat. As Bellany puts it: 'We were off the subs bench and onto the pitch in a flash!' Had it not been for the free travel, East Germany was the last place he would have gone. At that still-glacial period of the Cold War it was notorious for being the most hostile of all the Warsaw Pact countries.

Just how repressive it was was soon demonstrated in Dresden, where they had to have their Swinging Sixties locks shorn at the command of the music director. The irony did not escape them that throughout this operation they sat facing a bust of Karl Marx sporting a more leonine head of hair than they had ever dreamed of. After this sinister incident things improved.

The breakthrough came when Bellany charmed the wife of the Minister of Culture on the last night of the official programme. Undreamed-of doors opened. As one tour ended, another far more magical began – travel and accommodation no object – and this time organised entirely for their benefit. In Dresden John saw Otto Dix's *War* triptych and etchings which had as much of an impact on him as Goya's *Disasters of War*; in fact, he could have met Dix himself, but modesty forebore – a missed opportunity he regrets to this day. But he did meet Willi Sitte, President of the Artists Union, and the younger Werner Tubke, both socialist-realist painters of genuine power with no hint of the impersonal propaganda usually associated with the style. The English composer Alan Bush was in Germany at the same time. He befriended the three Scotsmen and was a constant source of support and encouragement during their stay.

Bellany's twenty-fifth birthday was celebrated in Berlin by seeing *The Threepenny Opera* performed by Brecht's own Berliner Ensemble, followed by a marathon club crawl. Friendship was consolidated with Barbara Brecht and her husband Eckehardt Schall, the director of the company and Brecht's son-in-law, twenty-five years later the subject of one of Bellany's best portraits of people other than his family. 'But 'the thunderbolt of all time' was the visit on a day of creeping fog to the site of the Buchenwald concentration camp.

With Sandy Moffat, 1967

Buchenwald means 'beech wood' and the camp was hidden in the depths of a forest. The huts had been removed but the concrete buildings remained on a great expanse of open ground, so large that in the mist its perimeter was invisible. There was a small museum documented with Teutonic thoroughness; but for Bellany the most horrific relic was the rusting machinery. The menacing presence of the Russian guards heightened the tension which reached a climax on the homeward journey, endured in stunned reflection, when a gigantic tank suddenly burst from the trees, forcing their bus to a skidding halt, before just as suddenly vanishing.

Buchenwald marked the true end of innocence for Bellany. Here was an opposite reality to the love he had been brought up to think of as a God-given right. At Buchenwald Hogg's nightmare had become reality. Now Bellany was convinced that a loving God could never have countenanced such evil. 'Hell obsessed him after Buchenwald', says Moffat. The stoical ancestors and fishermen were replaced by concentration-camp inmates, lost souls by the score. The most harrowing is the bitterly entitled *Resurrection* (1967), surely the most terrible crucifixion in British art, weirdly at odds with the fashion that year for the beads and bangles of Flower Power. It was a vision which seemed no longer applicable in the civilised west at that time but now appears disturbingly relevant again. Such dismay can also be more personally expressed. *The Fright* (1968) is a hellish vision of conjugal relations, a wildly expressive painting which had 'a big effect on later work'.

John Bellany at his degree exhibition, Edinburgh College of Art

Self-Portrait, 1967,
oil on board, 161 × 144CM,
63½ × 56¾IN.

My Grandmother, 1967,
crayon on paper, 55 x 38CM,
21¾ x 15IN.

The Fright, 1968, oil on board, 183 × 183CM, 72 × 72IN.

Scottish Family, 1968, oil on board, 243.5 × 160CM, 96 × 63IN.

Obsession, 1968, oil and collage on board, 243.5 × 160CM, 96 × 63IN.

Pourquoi?, 1967, oil on board, 200 × 212CM, 78¾ × 83½IN.

The Persecuted, 1967, oil on canvas, laid on board, 160 × 213.5CM, 63 × 84IN.

Pourquoi II?, 1967, oil on board, 173 × 180CM, 68 × 71IN.

Aujourd'hui, 1967, oil and collage on board, 198 × 326CM, 78 × 128IN.

The Persecuted, 1968, (detail), oil on board, 186 × 186CM, 73 × 73IN.

Self-Portrait with Jonathan, 1967, oil on board, 122 × 91.5CM, 48 × 36IN.
(Glasgow Museums: Art Gallery and Museum, Kelvingrove)

The Obsession (Whence do we come? Who are we? Whither do we go?), 1966, oil on board, 212 × 242.6CM, 83½ × 95½IN. (City Art Centre, Edinburgh)

The Bereaved One, 1968, oil on board, 91.5 × 91.5CM, 36 × 36IN. (The Scottish National Gallery of Modern Art)

Allegory, 1964, oil on board (triptych), 212.5 × 403.5CM, 83¾ × 158¾IN. (The Scottish National Gallery of Modern Art)

CHAPTER 6

Heavy Seas

John Bellany graduated from the Royal College in 1968 – 'covered in glory and honours' in Weight's phrase. His diploma show contained some of his most powerful paintings, among them *The Fright, Aujourd'hui* (painted over collaged cuttings from magazines, a rare contemporary touch), the first Buchenwald pictures and a few intense portraits of his favourite model, the bushy-haired *Antoinette*. It was a *tour de force*. Robin Philipson had already acknowledged the fact by exhibiting some of Bellany's early Royal College paintings at Edinburgh College of Art in 1968, several of them one day destined to enter the Tate, the Scottish National Gallery of Modern Art and other museum collections. Bellany returned the compliment by giving his old teacher and sparring partner one of the best of the *Buchenwald* series, *Lost Souls*, a gesture of gratitude that was to cement a friendship which continued until Philipson's death in 1993.

When Bellany graduated, Philipson offered him a full-time teaching job. It was tempting: Helen was pregnant with their second son Paul, Jonathan was three and they were living on a pittance. But Helen, to her credit, talked him out of it. Despite the harsh circumstances, they liked London; and settling for a cosy life in Scotland would have been a retreat – and a waste of time because she knew that, in Bellany's words, his 'artistic battleground' had been enlarged and was growing. Instead, he eventually found a less remunerative job of a day's teaching a week at the art college in Brighton. The biggest bonus was 'the glimpse of sea' as he walked from the station; but the job only lasted six months. He was too proud to register for social security or to ask for money, so a few odd jobs and the sale of one or two paintings had to pull them through. Teaching in art colleges would be his mainstay until the 1980s.

'It was a prestigious thing for an artist to do at that time. Since the 1980s the emphasis has changed to which gallery you are with and students no longer consider their time at art school an apprenticeship. They are encouraged to take short-cuts. They don't benefit from the slow build-up of a career, that cross-fertilisation we had, where we were all learning from each other not just about painting but about life.'

In 1968 Sonnie Maltman died. Bellany responded by painting *The Bereaved One* of his widowed grandmother. His love for her had already been enshrined in some of his most tender drawings. Now he painted her sitting lonely and defiant in the marital bed, the bedcovers like a river threatening to wash her away, the headboard a tombstone, a consoling bible open on her lap. His grandmother is one of several subjects Bellany has consistently returned to throughout his career.

This constant autobiographical impulse can become repetitive but is never self-indulgent. *The Bellany Family* (1968) is devoid of the complacent sentimentality usually associated with family portraits. John clutches a bottle of booze, while Helen, heavily pregnant, and Jonathan stare at the viewer along with victims of the Holocaust – in a picture within the picture. The presence of these victims and the sacrilegiously discarded bible, lying open amongst the jumble in the foreground, hint at despair. A toy parrot is the only glimmer of humour – anyone 'at sea' must have a parrot.

In 1969 Bellany painted his second major triptych, ironically entitled *Homage to John Knox*, the father of Scottish Calvinism and instigator of the religious oppression and iconoclasm the artist now found intolerable. It brought together the principal themes in his work at that time: the symbolic fishermen of *Kinlochbervie* (1966), a painting the artist Roberto Matta once perceptively told him 'he would paint again and again all his life';[23] the hopeless victims of *Lost Souls*; and overall the consciousness of the power of evil and the immanence of death.

The left panel depicts marriage as a prison imposed by the Church. The couple are chained together at the neck, the wife naked, the husband in the striped uniform of a concentration-camp prisoner. Three priest-like figures guard the bed, bearing symbols of marriage: a baby, a phallic fish and a bible. The right panel shows the Day of Judgment. The dead rise from their graves to be judged for their sins, one already in the air and seemingly condemned to the eternal fires of hell. Two lugubrious figures in cowls represent hell-fire sermonisers. These images of inner and outer darkness are contrasted with the daylit scene in the central panel of three men in a boat on a becalmed sea; but even they seem doomed. An owl and a raven – symbols of darkness – perch on the heads of two of the men; the third man sits hidden behind the humanoid 'mask' of a skate. The religious symbolism of this trio is emphasised by a bat hovering over the central figure and the sacrificial suggestion of the fish. A Goya-esque bat is substituted for the dove of the Holy Ghost, the fish for Christ; the two men to either side – one praying, the other playing the flute – are like attendant servers in a medieval altarpiece.

The design of this painting owes most to Beckmann's *Departure*; the device of the boat as a shallow barque with a net hanging diagonally over the side is derivative enough to constitute a

Painting Ian Botham at Birtles
Old Hall, Cheshire, 1985

Ian Botham, 1985,
oil on canvas, 173 × 152.5CM,
68 × 60IN.
(Courtesy of the National Portrait
Gallery, London)

deliberate act of deference. This was the consummation of his work in the 1960s and the last time he used hardboard, because of storage problems. He now began painting on canvas, which he found perplexing for the first six months until he got used to the 'tooth' of its surface. The change altered his technique. His use of glazes and meticulous handling were gradually replaced by a more modern and overtly expressionist style.

Initially Munch was the catalyst, William MacTaggart the younger (1903–81) was another Scottish painter inspired by the Norwegian, which may explain why Joanna Drew, ultimately director of the Hayward Gallery and Regional Exhibitions for the South Bank Centre and a former student of Edinburgh College of Art, sees Bellany in a Scottish tradition of painting, particularly associated with the younger MacTaggart and, later, Davie.

After Munch came Ensor, Bacon, Soutine, COBRA and Kokoschka. The sea and fishing remained a dominant theme but, as Keith Hartley has written, the emphasis switched 'from the world seen from without to the world seen from within. No longer would the fishermen and the fish-gutters be representatives from Port Seton, or of the world of work, but part of the debate in his own mind between such issues as life and death, good and evil, hope and fear.'[24]

A period of acute financial shortage was eased when Bellany was given a part-time teaching job one day a week at Winchester College of Art, extended to three days a week by 1972. Winchester rewarded the painter's spirit as well as his purse.[25] 'You know what art colleges are like. They hit the highspots for three or four years. I was lucky to go to Winchester as things there started to hit the highspots. If you have an enthusiastic staff and good students there's nothing better because everybody's learning – staff are learning from each other, students are learning from the staff – and that really broadened my understanding enormously.'

Trevor Bell was head of fine art, Scottish-bred William Crozier was head of painting and Heinz Hengis was head of sculpture. Hengis, an older man, had known Kandinsky and Brancusi. There were also numerous visiting artists, among them the painters Patrick Heron and Harry Mundy.

'Everyone was trying as hard as hell in their different directions and yet there was this camaraderie of being artists. I had previously been a bit evangelistic – "This is the only way" – but I now realised that people could express themselves in totally different ways and yet still be as dedicated and sincere as I was. It taught me a bit of humility and increased my erudition.'

The change is so marked between Bellany's early work on hardboard and the subsequent canvases that it amounts to a choice. His teachers, perhaps inevitably, prefer the early work and so do those, like his son Jonathan, whose taste is for something more simple. Certainly the early work taken as a whole has a concentrated power that remains unmatched. Canvas has encouraged greater speed and for a compulsive painter this has led to greater dependence on spontaneity and a higher failure rate. 'Death is always just round the corner,' he told W. Gordon Smith in a BBC TV documentary on his life and work in 1974. 'At thirty-two?' questioned his old interviewer. 'Yes. Maybe it's impatience but I just want to pack my life. I've always got to be testing myself all the time.'

Bellany's post-1970 output certainly requires more editing, as the artist freely admits. In the same interview he says he was making between two and three hundred paintings a year, having 'to paint a dozen to get a beauty'.

'He's highly productive, like me,' says Alan Davie, 'and we can't be expected to get it right every time!' Selection has not always been sufficiently rigorous and some secondary paintings have been shown or have received the greatest publicity for the wrong reasons, like his portrait of Ian Botham or the widely displayed and popular posters of *Chinatown* and *Camden Lock* for the London Underground.

At Winchester Bellany learned etching, a medium ideally suited to his skill for drawing and the dark mood of his subject matter. As a student at Edinburgh he had found it 'dreary, like being taught gardening' (an activity he has always avoided); but when Norman Ackroyd, who taught printmaking, saw some of Bellany's drawings he suggested he had a go. 'He was an obvious etcher because there was so much drawing in his painting. Good painters are natural etchers. Also he's a very spontaneous painter and etching is a spontaneous medium. I only had to suggest it to John and he just went for it. He didn't nibble about on the plate. He's a terrific etcher.'

Two plates were prepared and Ackroyd told him to draw on them just as he would on a piece of paper. The results were *The Burden*, a man with a fish on his back,[26] and *The Scapegoat* (1970), now both in the Tate Collection. *The Burden* was particularly significant, inspiring several paintings and the memorable photographic portrait by Snowdon on the cover of this book.

His early etchings are a tantalising combination of hair's-breadth delicacy and moody description, in parallel with his painting. 'Every year since, I've done loads of them. I love the sensuality of it, the feeling of drawing into the ground. And then I got into the various techniques – open bite, sugar lift – through my own excitement and wish to extend my range.' Etching affected his painting, introducing a greater clarity, 'because it's got to be right first time'.

That same year he had his first one-man exhibition in London, at Halima Nalecz's Drian Gallery, where he showed regularly until the late 1970s. The introduction came through Winchester in the person of William Crozier. 'I liked John's work immediately because it was authentic, which is all that matters,' says Nalecz. 'It took courage to show him because his paintings take time to appreciate and he is one of

John and Helen Bellany with Tim Hudson at Eversden, two weeks after returning from hospital

Mr Tim Hudson, 1985, oil on canvas, 152.5 × 152.5CM, 60 × 60IN. (Courtesy The National Portrait Gallery, London)

the most difficult artists for the public. You have to select carefully. I find his recent work a bit overcrowded, I prefer it more simple, but he is a marvellous painter, a very great talent.'

'Halima Nalecz was a tremendous support and enthusiast,' says Bellany. The only problem at Drian was size, the gallery being too small to take his larger works. But it was here he got his start. Douglas Hall, frustrated from buying a Bellany at this date by his trustees, bought *Gates of Death* (1970) for the Scottish Arts Council collection from his first show; and the Arts Council of Great Britain bought *The Voyage* (1973) from his third. Halima Nalecz also presented seven of his large works to public collections in Poland, most prestigiously the National Gallery in Warsaw.

Bellany's literary erudition had meanwhile come on apace, enriching the work particularly through his enthusiasm for French poetry and novels, principally those by Céline, Camus, Sartre and Gide. Clarity encouraged by etching was reinforced by self-expressive gesture. In a Munchian swirl of 'nothingness', figures are marooned in existential isolation. As always, Bellany's art speaks with the conviction of personal experience.

He had gained the freedom of a separate 'studio', above a tailor's shop at 164 Battersea High Street, which he shared with Norman Ackroyd. They were on three months notice but the rent was token and the space – two floors of two rooms each – gave John more room, at least until his separation from Helen in 1974. Occupation was another matter. There was no hot running water and, because one room was chock-a-block with pictures, he had to eat, sleep, paint and put up the children at the weekends in one fifteen-by-twenty-foot room. The roof leaked intermittently, once giving Paul 'a real christening' in the middle of the night, and it was verminous. In Bellany's description it was 'a wee dump', a black chapter reflected in a dark and fiery palette and brooding subject matter.

'I think a lot of people would have given up and taken another job,' says Jonathan. Perhaps Bellany was sustained by the thought of his own father's hardships as a fisherman, the tales of trips before the war when Dick Bellany might return to Port Seton from three months' fishing out of Lowestoft and Great Yarmouth with nothing to show for it; 'and living on that wee boat all of that time, it's amazing how they did it'. But for all the misery of Battersea, Bellany preferred working there to a much larger space he was offered in an industrial building near the heliport.

The house was condemned but Ackroyd and Bellany had the use of it throughout the 1970s. 'What we shared was a Calvinistic work ethic: the work had to be banked before you could enjoy yourself,' remembers Ackroyd, who dispels the notion that Bellany was in any way hampered by drink at this point. 'We were very respectful of each other's privacy – some days all we'd do would be to shout hello through the door. We never drank at lunchtime. It was incredibly professional. Hordes of people came to our "open studios". I was worried the floors would collapse. They never bought much. John used to call them our "invisible earnings". When you did go on a bender with John, of course, it was always outrageous. He held very strong opinions and when he was drunk he could be abusive, especially if something like Warhol came up. He is essentially very gentle but I think he did put a lot of people off.'

Bellany's drinking was not yet legendary but it was heading that way. Joanna Drew has an earlier memory of Peter de Francia leaving her with Bellany and Alan Bold, both the worse for drink. They were too far gone to find their way home so she put them to bed. In the morning she found them 'looking like Pooh and Piglet and still just as drunk as they had been the night before!' As Carel Weight put it: 'Like lots of Scots he was rather fond of the bottle.' No doubt Warhol's name came up in Exeter, from where Bellany was banned by the police for a year at some point in that confused decade.

In retrospect Bellany thinks taking a separate studio was the greatest mistake of his life because it meant he was not spending enough time with his family. The truth is he did not have the time for steady fatherhood, for all that the children still fondly remember his cavorting with the accordion and helping them to make toy boats. After Anya's birth in September 1970, Helen was mostly left to cope on her own: 'Life was exciting for him and he was meeting lots of new people, whereas domestic life was a hindrance.' This drift led to a separation in 1974 and divorce in 1978.

John Bellany seems to paint in three-year cycles and from 1970 to 1973 the mood is definitely hellish. Backgrounds suggest molten brimstone and he is precociously tormented by death. In *Madonna* (1971) Christian iconography is subverted by the bitterly ironic image of a pregnant woman plagued by guilt. Instead of a religious icon in the shrine above her bed there is the mocking figure of a rampant ram, surrounded by flames of desire. *The Fishers* (1972) is a variation on the central panel of *Homage to John Knox*, but the emphasis is very different. The skate is not held here as an offering but as a familiar, a human replacement and source of consolation. The style reverts to the stiff formalism of the 1960s after the expressionist fluidity of *The Burden*, but it was fluidity which he would now pursue.

The death of his grandmother in 1972 represented another anchor gone. 'She epitomised such goodness, a person in a permanent state of grace; and suddenly she was no longer there. Life seemed to be running away with me. It was like living fifty years in one year, that kind of intensity. Through immaturity and stupidity, though it's always easy to understand these things in retrospect, I think I mucked it up. Things went too far wrong and the further they went the thirstier I got'.

Drinking was still a convivial matter of 'spreeing' of an evening, and his painting style assumed a new clarity and fluidity; nevertheless, his 1972 self-portrait *You're 30 Today, John* painted on his birthday – a practice he has maintained ever since – shows his head bandaged like Van Gogh's and half his ribcage illuminated as if by an X-ray. He seems only partially belonging to this world as he sits in a huddle, wounded and insecure, at what might be the doors to hell.

The power of Bellany's work is driven by the honesty with which he has depicted his own experience, no matter what the disgust or physical impracticality. 'You can't paint from a vacuum. Whether you're in a state of serenity or absolute anguish like I was living, if you're being honest it comes through in the work.' But there is also his talent for drawing: 'I had a memorable conversation on New Year's Night 1973 at the Kismet Club in Soho with Francis Bacon about the drawing in the painting of Michelangelo. I find it difficult to believe that Bacon didn't do drawings because he spoke with such passion and expertise on drawing being the core of painting; in the way drawing with paint is the same as in pencil. Drawing is drawing. In my view there's more drawing in a Pollock than in any dreary life drawing or portrait study by the academic duds one sees round the world. There is a fundamental misunderstanding about what drawing is, what drawing does and what drawing means.'

There is more than a hint of Bacon in the way Bellany's painting of the early 1970s tacks between dark despair and radiant interludes of calm; the power and delusion of sex, and the fear of death from its sinful consequences, continue to fever his imagination. Ominous presences abound, all is sin, guilt and remorse, and marriage is a mockery. *Lobster Fetish* (1971) shows a woman as lobster bait. The lobster, its creepy carnality emphasised by the weblike fragility of the restraining string, is caught in the pot and seems in the process of feasting on her heart. A dog – 'god' spelt backwards – surveys the gruesome sacrifice.

Subjection to powers beyond mortal control is a dominant theme in 1972–73. *Obsession* (1973) returns to the subject of marriage as enslavement alluded to in *Homage to John Knox*. The sacrificial symbol of a sheep is placed between the chained marital couple; the man is in the absurd form of a puffin, a self-mocking image created at this time. Masks confer specific attributes to his figures. As with all symbolism they are a descriptive shorthand and slowly subsume the human figure so that by the late 1970s, in a painting like *The Voyagers* (1977), humans disappear to be replaced by bird, fish and dog.

In *Celtic Feast II* (1973) three figures crouch down round a strange and unappetising dish of a dog, a fish and a giant snail. The masked male figure has two female companions, one symbolic of loyalty and the other, provocatively naked, of desire. The painting has a calming serenity of design, heraldic in its symmetry and rhyming use of stripes and chevron; disturbing Munchian flux is confined to a corner. The room is meticulously clean and uncluttered, unlike the studio in which it was painted: 'It was real squalor, no hot water, vermin-infested; and I've got a phobia for mice and rats and things. It was absolutely hideous; and instead of getting out of it, it was like a malignancy, a course of self-destruction.'

Who would think Bellany had a care in the world from the delightful photograph on the cover of the catalogue for the show at the Drian Gallery in the autumn of 1973? He smiles as he plays the accordion with Anya on his shoulders and Paul and Jonathan grinning either side, all of them with the shoulder-length hair fashionable at the time. Two supportive and perceptive essays by Eddie Wolfram and William Crozier introduced the catalogue. 'Thus far Bellany is one of the real forerunners of tomorrow's trend, as soon as it dawns in fashionable circles that from now on any meaningful new art is going to be more a question of *derrière-garde* rather than continuing to plough through arid and trivial innovations with ephemeral materials and soft-headed quasi-philosophical ideas,' wrote Wolfram prophetically.[27] In 1973 the Arts Council bought *The Voyage*, painted the same year, his first picture to enter a major public collection.

The final break-up of the marriage came in 1974. From Helen's point of view it was a case of self-preservation: 'I thought I was literally going mad at times with loneliness,' she says.

Bellany suffered a nervous breakdown and had to withdraw to Port Seton for six months to stay with his parents. Like Job he could have said his soul was weary of his life.[28] For weeks he never left the cave-like darkness and security of his bedroom and for a short time was unable to work – a unique experience. But, as usual, his urge to paint and draw proved irresistible. On the beach one day he picked up a razor shell, the inspiration of *Self-Portrait with Razor Shell*. But he recognises that it was the love his family showed which really pulled him through. 'It's like longevity. You think you'll live forever. With a crack up, you think it'll never happen to you and then – snap – it does. I think things like that are much worse than any physical illness.'

Drian Galleries

5-7 PORCHESTER PLACE, MARBLE ARCH, LONDON, W.2
Telephone 01-723 9473

JOHN BELLANY

Cover of the catalogue for the 1971 exhibition of drawings and etchings at Drian Galleries, London

The Bellany family, 1973

Ominous Presence, 1973, oil on canvas, 213.5 × 192.5CM, 84 × 75¾IN.

Lovers, 1969, oil on board, 213.5 × 183CM, 84 × 72IN.

The Bellany Family, 1968, oil on board, 183 × 244CM, 72 × 96IN.
(Reproduced by permission of Perth & Kinross District Council, Museum and Art Galleries Department, Scotland)

Homage to John Knox, 1969, oil on board, 244 × 480CM, 96 × 189IN. (Oslo Museum)

The Burden, 1970,
etching (edition of 75), paper size 75 × 75CM,
29½ × 29½IN.

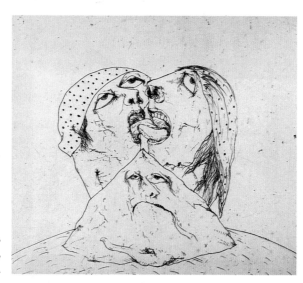

The Kiss I, 1970,
etching (edition of 50), paper size 64.5 × 50CM,
25½ × 22IN.

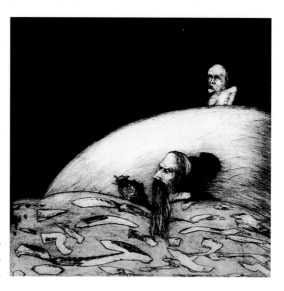

Death Knell for John Knox, 1970,
etching (edition of 75), paper size 75 × 75CM,
29½ × 29½IN.

The Family, 1970, oil on board, 213.5 × 183CM, 84 × 72IN.

Self-Portrait, 1971, oil on canvas, 156 × 120.5CM, 61½ × 47½IN.

Lobster Fetish, 1971, oil on canvas, 177 × 187CM, 69¾ × 73½IN.

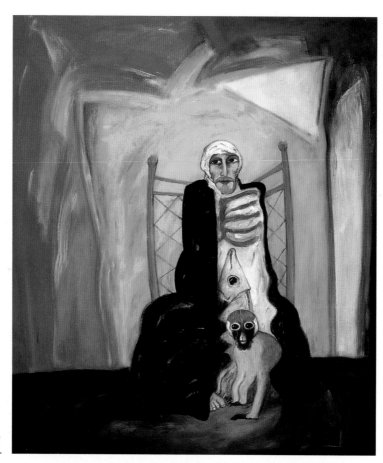

You're 30 Today, John, 1972,
oil on canvas, 175 × 161CM, 69 × 63½IN.

Woman with Skate, 1972,
oil on canvas, 217 × 184CM,
85½ × 72½IN.

Celtic Supper, 1973,
oil on canvas, 185 × 185CM,
73 × 73IN.

Sacrifice II, 1973,
oil on canvas, 188 × 183CM,
74 × 72IN.

Celtic Feast, 1973/74, oil on canvas (triptych), 188 × 360CM, 74 × 142IN. (Collection Mappin Art Gallery, Sheffield)

Skate Fetish, 1973, oil on canvas,
206 × 191CM, 81 × 75IN.

Celtic Sacrifice, 1973, oil on canvas,
180 × 161CM, 71 × 63½IN.

The Fish God Cometh, 1970/71,
oil on canvas, 205 × 187CM,
80¾ × 73½IN.

Lap Dog, c.1973,
oil on canvas, 185 × 165CM,
73 × 65IN.
(The Scottish National Gallery of Modern Art)

Self-Portrait with Accordion, 1974, oil on canvas, 172.5 × 152.5CM, 68 × 60IN.

The Sea People, 1975, oil on canvas, 246.5 × 183CM, 97 × 72IN. (Collection The Arts Council of Great Britain)

Journey to the End of the Night, 1972, oil on canvas (triptych), 209.9 × 460.5CM, 82½ × 181IN.
(Glasgow Museums: Art Gallery and Museum, Kelvingrove)

Self-Portrait with Razor Shell, 1976, oil on canvas, 183 × 168CM, 72 × 66IN.
(Scottish Arts Council Collection)

Cod End, 1977, oil on canvas (triptych), 198 × 247CM, 78 × 97IN.

The Accordionist, 1978,
oil on board, 183 x 161CM, 72 x 63½IN.

You an' me in oor creel again, 1979, oil on canvas, 254 × 127CM, 100 × 50IN.

Mizpah, 1978, oil on canvas, 243.8 × 243.8CM (Collection Scottish National Gallery of Modern Art)

CHAPTER 7
Down the Hatch

On his return to London Bellany had a lucky break. He managed to rent a little house in World's End, Chelsea. He thought it looked like Van Gogh's house in Arles but because it was white with dark blue windows and the Scotland football team was in the World Cup his children christened it the Scottish Embassy. The accommodation was still very basic – no bath and only a small hot-water unit – but there were four rooms and a double garage in which he could store his paintings. The children continued to stay every weekend.

Like many Scots they were all 'fitba' crazy'. Through the 1970s and early 1980s their greatest treat was to see Chelsea or, supreme event, the England *v* Scotland match. Bellany painted his hip-bath blue in honour of club and country. His son Paul remembers: 'Even if we were only watching the Scotland match on TV we'd have the whole place covered in scarves and Scottish flags and he'd probably have bought a tartan shirt specially for the occasion, as he was into it as much as anyone else. And we always watched *Match of the Day* on the TV on Saturday nights.' Paul lavished his own artistic talent on drawing and writing his own football magazine. Willie Ormond was not the family's only privileged contact with the game; one of the Bellanys, his cousin Arthur, was a scout for Celtic, and had been capped for Scotland.

In 1975 Bellany had a major exhibition at Aberdeen Art Gallery, which was accompanied by W. Gordon Smith's TV documentary. To paint primarily to make a living was anathema to him. He brooked no compromise. Painting was not a matter of supply and demand; it was a quest for inner truth. Nonetheless, a sale was a bonus and sales did improve. It should not be forgotten how relatively cheap pictures were, and how unfashionable – despite the growing awareness of the equation of art and money due to the success of the auction houses.

From 1973 to 1978 Bellany was head of the faculty of painting at Croydon College of Art, where his colleagues included David Royle, Denis Bowen, Barry Martin and the late Mel Gordon. It was at this time that he became a close friend of the abstract-expressionist painter Albert Irvin. They had first met when Bellany was at the Royal College and Irvin selected his *Three Fishermen* for a London Group exhibition. Bellany invited Irvin to teach painting at Croydon on a part-time basis, a compliment later returned when he left Croydon and Irvin found him a job at Goldsmiths College of Art.

Bellany met Juliet Lister through his work at Croydon. She was a great-niece of Lord Lister, who discovered antiseptics, and was older than Bellany, a mature student studying sculpture. They married in 1979, buying a house in Windmill Drive in Clapham Common. By then he had moved to Goldsmiths College of Art as Lecturer in Painting. His work at Goldsmiths amounted to two days' teaching a week which he augmented with a day at the Royal College, leaving him four days a week for his own work – a balance which served him well when he was still unable to live off his painting.

In 1978 and 1979 he managed to have four shows each year, including an exhibition initiated by the Third Eye Centre in Glasgow, which travelled to Newcastle Polytechnic Art Gallery and Southampton City Art Gallery. Dr David Brown, formerly Douglas Hall's assistant in Edinburgh, but now assistant keeper of the Modern Collection at the Tate, was advisor on purchases for the Southampton gallery. Bellany had given him some 'verbal abuse' at an opening on the subject of the Tate's neglect of his work. As a result Brown visited his studio and was impressed, returning at a later date with the director, Sir Norman Reid, a Scot, and Richard Morphet, deputy keeper of the Modern Collection. Reid and Morphet were equally impressed, Reid reserving *Celtic Marriage* (1978) on the spot.

Bellany remembers that Reid almost preferred *You an' me in oor creel again* (1979), a tougher painting in his opinion, one of his most abstract at that date. Reid and his wife Jean had met when pupils of Edinburgh College of Art, and Reid was 'touched' to find an artist whose work was inspired by a part of Scotland which he himself held in such affection. Jean Reid also became an enthusiast and, when she met Bellany, was particularly struck by the regard in which he held his father.

At this time the Contemporary Art Society wanted to purchase a work for the Tate's permanent collection to celebrate the opening of the new extension. The Tate decided to buy one of Bellany's early works. Brown proposed *Bethel* (1967), the painting he still considers Bellany's masterpiece; but as the painting needed some conservation work which could not be done in time they bought *Star of Bethlehem* (1968) instead. Brown meanwhile bought *Bethel* for Southampton. The price was £1,100.

The Tate's tardiness in recognising Bellany's work is characteristic of public patrons, who are notoriously cautious compared to the private collector, most decisions having to be agreed by a committee. Nonetheless, Bellany's obscurity in the 1970s also played a part in his lack of recognition. Nor did the size of his work help, particularly that of the intractable hardboard paintings. Douglas Hall would have liked to have bought one of these but Inverleith House in Edinburgh was too small. The first work by the painter to be bought by the National Gallery of Modern Art was *Mizpah* (1978) in 1980. Amends have since been made to the tune of forty-seven gifts or purchases.

Teaching was a particular feature of Bellany's life in the 1970s. 'He loved students,' says Michael Craig-Martin, who was on the staff at Goldsmiths. Bellany always treated teaching as a challenge, just as he enjoyed challenging fellow artists to draw him while he drew them. If he was invited to an art school he would insist on being provided with the means to paint alongside the students. His spontaneous approach as a teacher once got him into trouble when he decided on the spur of the moment to take his class to France for the day. He got them to draw the passengers on the hovercraft during the crossing, presenting each one with the resulting portrait at the end of the trip.

John Bellany's second wife, Juliet, with her mother, 1982

At Goldsmiths the apparent enmity between painters and neo-conceptualists provided, according to the conceptually inclined Michael Craig-Martin, a fruitful clash of opinion: 'It was the policy of Goldsmiths for the staff to be as outspoken as possible. There was never a consensus. The idea that has arisen that it was single-mindedly neo-conceptual is nonsense. Everybody was encouraged to fight their corner. That's why John liked it. Personally, I love people who are intensely themselves and no one could have been more intensely himself than John.'

As Helen says, his most perpetual refrain has been: 'We're not just messing about. We're taking on the world.' But in general the art world treated him with caution. 'No one would touch him,' remembers Monika Kinley, who was his agent – 'his "special agent" he used to call me' – from 1978 until 1985. His drinking was to blame. It was not that it made him violent – 'to his credit he was always gentle,' says Kinley, 'and often very funny in his cups' – but he was 'difficult'. 'To go out with John meant you were going to lose two days of your life,' says Bert Irvin. Sandy Moffat agrees: 'When John was drinking it was an ordeal.'

Increasingly drink made him ill, and an unreliable prospect when trying to ingratiate buyers. This was not improved by marriage to Juliet, a sweet-natured person – 'more of a friend than a step-mother,' as Anya Bellany testifies – but whose health was even more precarious than his. To an outsider she was a secret in his life, largely because she was so often unwell; and in his many paintings of her she is often a veiled or half-hidden figure. Their life together was blighted by her manic depression which required frequent periods in hospital. But at the beginning the romance inspired a series of light and airy paintings, their marriage seen characteristically as a voyage. *Mizpah* (1978) is a distinguished example. The title derives from the famous Eyemouth boat of that name, in turn taken from Genesis, chapter 31, verse 48–49:

Chinatown poster commissioned by London Underground

And Laban said, This heap is a witness between me and thee this day. Therefore was the name of it called Galeed;

And Mizpah; for he said, The Lord watch between me and thee, when we are absent from another.

Bellany wears the fool's motley of a puffin mask and is playing an accordion inscribed with the words 'lune de miel'; Juliet is a seagull in wedding white; a celebratory offering of a crucified heap of fish stands over them. *Mizpah* is the name of the boat on which they embark for their new life together. The word meant a great deal to them. It stood as the symbol of their love.

Bellany's increasing freedom in handling the paint was encouraged by his discovery of watercolour, as important a discovery as etching had been. Until then he had not seriously considered watercolour, but while staying one weekend at Hastings with the painter Gus Cummins and his wife Angie, it was suggested he try. He was given a sketchpad and miniature box of paints and became so engrossed by the medium that he reeled off half a dozen paintings that first afternoon. Since then he has produced many watercolours, making it as essential a part of his *oeuvre* as did earlier expressionist painters like Nolde and Kokoschka. For an artist who paints so many subjects related to water it is a metaphor in itself and he uses it with great empathy. His washes are tinctured as delicately as the bloody water on a fishmonger's slab, his application as speedily controlled as a gutting.

During his time at Goldsmiths, Bellany developed a deep friendship with the artists Harry and Elma Thubron. Among their countless escapades was one memorable trip to France, which Bellany remembers as 'a blend of Pernod, watercolours, singing tributes to Oscar Wilde and Sickert, endless moules marinières and the usual hearty laughter and banter'.

In 1979 Bellany was invited to represent Britain in the Independent Irish Artists Exhibition in Dublin, along with Francis Bacon, Lucian Freud and William Crozier. After a rollicking lunch in his honour at the Chelsea Arts Club given by Carel Weight, Robert Buhler and William Scott, Bellany flew off for the opening in the highest spirits, only to make the dismaying discovery after the plane was airborne that he had got the dates muddled and was arriving one week early. 'That's your bad news but I've got worse,' said the passenger to whom he had confided his distress, 'it's a bank holiday weekend.' However, the web of contacts he had made through teaching stood him in good stead and he passed a memorable 'lost weekend' as a guest of Campbell Bruce, head of painting at Dublin College of Art. On a stroll round Dublin harbour he drew a rusting hulk. The latest talking-point was of another IRA atrocity, and the certainty and prosperity of the world the old ship had been launched into seemed to have decayed no less woefully. The result was the painting *L'Age d'Or*, a key work for him in its simultaneously comforting and harrowing way, which subsequently won a prize at the John Moores Liverpool Exhibition that year.

Bellany's personal life was also washed up. Juliet's ill-health doomed the marriage. She would often lie in bed for days while he drank recklessly, not 'the amber nectar' but Bacardi rum, the sailor's grog. The children did their best, watering down or emptying his hidden bottles, but it was useless. They recognised a new stage had been reached when, on one of their annual and treasured visits to Port Seton, they noticed their father hiding his habit from his parents.

'Very occasionally he'd take it out on us but although drink may have stopped us getting closer to him, he was never violent. He very rarely ever seemed drunk. He'd always be the life and soul of the party,' says Paul. 'What I liked was he didn't care about convention. He wasn't obnoxious, it was just a case of "Let's have fun, whatever people think".'

With David Bowie, Edinburgh

One New Year's Eve they were all out on Clapham Common as the clocks struck midnight, kicking a football in the snow, Bellany playing the accordion and football all at the same time. Domesticity was not his strong point. The art critic Mary Rose Beaumont was shocked by the chaos of the house but became a staunch friend.

That Bellany recognised his predicament is reflected in the growing agitation of his brushstrokes, his subjects and titles: *The Gambler* (1981), *Walking the Plank* (1982), *Time Will Tell* (1982). The figure of a clock, as if he is painting against time, becomes an insistent symbol. In *Self-Portrait with Juliet* (1980), he is half-hidden by a grandfather clock while she peeps out from behind a book. The crisis of self-confidence and self-identity is made even more explicit by the drawing *Self-Portrait Looking over Back of Chair* (1981), in which MacDiarmid's famous line 'To be yersel' is ruefully obliterated by a fierce cross-hatch of lines. The job of being himself can never have seemed more dispiriting. This frustration is equally evident in *Shipwreck* (1982) which verges on the abstract-expressionism of de Kooning in its aggression; a wheel of fortune dimly, ironically, visible, *The Ventriloquist* (1983) shows a skeleton in a boat holding up two dead skate.

Ominous Presence, 1971/72, oil on canvas, 213.5 × 198CM, 84 × 78IN. (Collection David Bowie)

His ability to express himself at this desperate time resulted in some of his most searching and painful works. With hindsight it is disgraceful that he was not included in the Royal Academy's 'A New Spirit in Painting' exhibition of 1981. This was a significant event because it confirmed the return of expressionism to market-favour after two decades fashionably dominated by art in which emotion was rigorously avoided, starting with Pop and ending in the verbal conceits of conceptualism. Among younger painters Bellany had kept the expressionist flag flying as vigorously as George Baselitz had in

Valhalla, oil on board (triptych), 80 × 130IN. (Collection David Bowie)

My Father, 1978,
oil on canvas, 178 × 183CM,
70 × 72IN.
(Collection Richard Zeisler)

Germany, whom he acknowledges as a fellow spirit. But the show was paid for by the West German government with the obvious purpose of reconciling Germany with the rebirth of expressionism – previously *verboten* as the malignant root of German nationalism – both with modern Germany and her former enemies. The politics inherent in large international exhibitions demands the clout of vested interest rendering a solo operator like Bellany expendable. However, that year he did at least receive a major Arts Council award.

On the basis of this windfall and the offer of a lavish show in Los Angeles he took a sabbatical from Goldsmiths. The Los Angeles exhibition failed to materialise but this was more than compensated for when Monika Kinley arranged his first show in New York, early in 1982, at the Rosa Esman Gallery. Thanks to the generosity of the English painter John Walker, who lent him his upstate studio, Bellany was also able to do some oils. They were the 'wildest' of his life, perhaps reflecting the impact of seeing the greatest works of the abstract-expressionists at first-hand in the cauldron of the city of their making. Rory McEwen, who would die later that year from cancer, also had an exhibition and the two Berwickshire-bred artists met for the first and last time, spending several enjoyably nostalgic sessions, surprising orphans of a common storm.

Rosa Esman sold works to several important American collectors including Richard Zeisler, a trustee of both the Museum of Modern Art and the Metropolitan Museum. Bellany was unprepared for the spectacle which greeted him when he visited Zeisler's apartment for the first time in 1987: 'I walked in and it was incredible: a fabulous Soutine, a Picasso, a Rouault, a Delvaux, all of them famous examples. And then I turned round and there on the opposite wall was my Dad! – the painting *My Father* done in 1978. Round the corner was *My Son Jonathan* painted the same year in between masterpieces by Matisse and Chagall. What a thrill it was, especially as I was by then chronically ill.' The Zeisler collection has since been bequeathed to the Museum of Modern Art.

That same year, 1983, Bellany was offered the honorarium of artist-in-residence at Victoria College of the Arts, Melbourne, for the summer semester, an opportunity set up by John Walker, who was dividing his time between teaching in Australia and New York.

Bellany's arrival in Australia coincided with a holiday celebrating the first day of spring. Despite feeling like death after his flight, he was persuaded to go to a party in the country at the house of the Australian artist Clifton Pugh. After 'a few heart starters *en route*' he picked up a bit and revived even quicker once he arrived, meeting 'all the Australian hierarchy in one fell swoop', who welcomed him like a brother. He enjoyed himself so much that he stayed the night. 'I went out like a light but at some point I was woken up by this awful retching noise – "Whoa!! Whoooaaar!" – terrible! I thought: "What on earth's that?" It never struck me I wasn't still in London, you see. So I opened my eyes and here were these horrific hairy great birds strolling past! "Oh no!" I thought, "I've had it! It's the DTs! It's finally caught up with me!" And I just pulled the blanket over my head and blacked out. Next thing this strange man's waking me up – Clifton Pugh. He asked me if I'd slept all right. So I told him what a fright I'd had in the middle of the night. "Oh," he says, "that was only my emus!"' *Only an Emu Passing By* (1983) commemorates this surreal incident.

After passing this trial by fire he never looked back: 'I was welcomed as a real "brother of the brush" by the Australian art community.' Friendships with Sydney Nolan and Jeff Makin were among those forged and Lynn Williams did him the honour of presenting him with the razor of her late husband, Fred Williams. The light in Australia, particularly the atmospheric purity of Perth, captivated him, and he produced enough work – including the outstanding *Totentanz* (1983) – to have three solo exhibitions in the three major centres of art: Melbourne, Sydney and Perth.

With Richard Zeisler at Keiss Castle, Caithness, 1991

My Son Jonathan, 1978,
oil on canvas, 183 × 183CM, 72 × 72IN.
(Collection Richard Zeisler)

Self-Portrait with Juliet, 1979, oil on canvas, 208 × 164CM, 82 × 64½IN.

Juliet, 1979,
oil on board, 183 × 62CM,
72 × 24½IN.

Juliet, 1979, oil on canvas,
194 × 124CM,
76½ × 49IN.

Sad Self-Portrait, 1976, oil on canvas, 210.5 × 165CM, 83 × 65IN.

Fidelas, 1981, oil on canvas (triptych), 172.5 × 305CM, 68 × 120IN.

The Voyagers II, 1982, oil on canvas, 122 × 173CM, 48 × 68IN.

Cockenzie Man Laments the Shipwreck, 1982, oil on canvas (diptych), 172.5 × 305CM, 68 × 120IN.

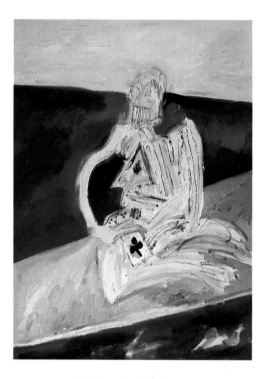

Celtic Encounter, 1982,
oil on canvas, 173 × 122CM,
68 × 48IN.

Walking the Plank, 1982,
oil on canvas, 172.5 × 122CM,
68 × 48IN.

The Gambler, 1981,
oil on canvas, 173 × 152.5CM,
68 × 60IN.
(Collection The Arts Council of Great Britain)

The Drinker, 1982,
oil on canvas, 172.5 × 122CM,
68 × 48IN.

Encounter, 1982/83, oil on canvas, 213 × 167.5CM, 84 × 66IN.

If music be the food of love, play on, 1983, oil on canvas (diptych), 213 × 328CM, 85 × 131IN.

Lune de Miel, 1983, oil on canvas (triptych), 213.5 × 363CM, 84 × 143IN.

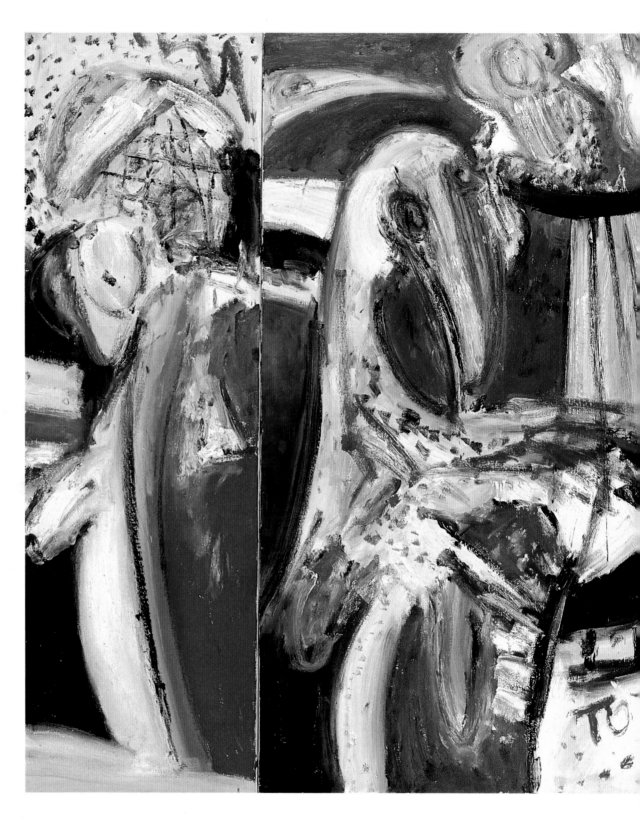

Totentanz, 1983, oil on canvas (triptych), 182 × 272CM, 71½ × 107IN.

Homage to Fred Williams, 1983, oil on canvas, 152.5 × 183CM, 60 × 72IN.

The Gambler, 1983,
oil on canvas, 152.5 × 183CM,
60 × 72IN.

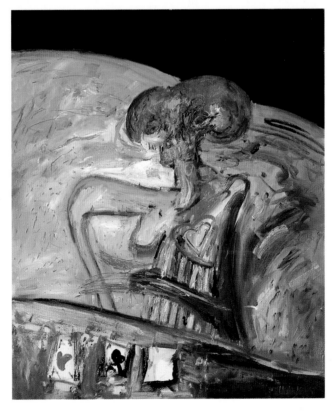

Tightrope of Life, 1983,
oil on canvas, 213 × 213CM,
84 × 84IN.

The Kiss of Life, 1984,
oil on canvas, 172.5 × 152.5CM,
68 × 60IN.

Accordionist I, 1984,
oil on canvas, 173 × 152.5CM,
68 × 60IN.

Ominous Presence, 1984,
oil on canvas, 173 × 152.5CM,
68 × 60IN.

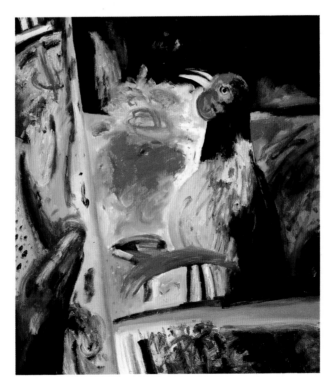

Capercaillie Sings His Love Song, 1984,
oil on canvas, 172.5 × 152.5CM,
68 × 60IN.

Time and the Raven, 1982, oil on canvas, 172.5 × 172.5CM, 68 × 68 IN.

Sea Cat, 1984,
oil on canvas, 213.5 × 172.5CM,
84 × 68IN.

Untitled, 1984,
ink on paper, 75.5 × 57CM,
30 × 22IN.

Helen, 1985, oil on canvas, 152.5 × 152.5CM, 60 × 60IN. (Courtesy The National Portrait Gallery, London)

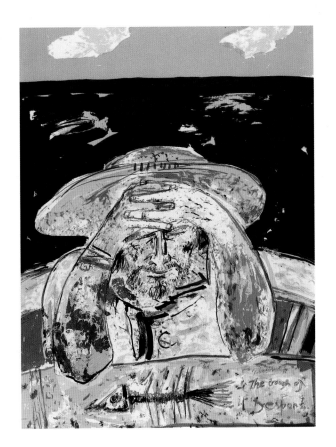

3 × Untitled, 1987, from 'The Old Man and the Sea' portfolio, 76 × 56.5CM, 30 × 22¼IN.

The Trough of Despont, 1987, from 'The Old Man and the Sea' portfolio, screenprint, 77 × 57CM, 30¼ × 22½IN.
(Collection Museum of Modern Art, New York)

Ventriloquist, 1983, oil on canvas, 181.1 × 151.5CM, 72¼ × 60½ IN.

*The Artist Holds the
Bird of Paradise*, 1985,
oil on canvas, 152.5 × 122CM,
60 × 48IN.

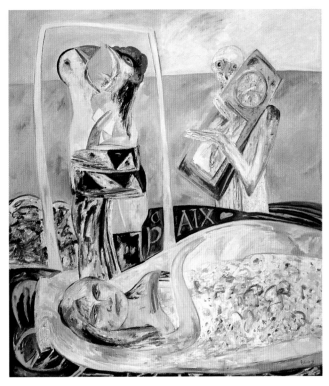

A Paix, 1986,
oil on canvas, 173 × 153CM,
68 × 60IN.

Bonaventure, 1986, watercolour, 76 × 56CM, 30 × 22IN. (Whitworth Art Gallery, University of Manchester)

Whence do we come,
Whither do we go?, 1986,
oil on canvas, 172.5 × 152.5CM,
68 × 60IN.

Sean Connery, 1986,
oil on canvas, 152.5 × 122CM,
60 × 48IN.
(Scottish National Portrait Gallery)

Achates, 1987, watercolour on paper, 76 × 57.5CM, 30 × 22IN.

The Pianist, 1987,
oil on canvas, 213.5 × 172.5CM, 84 × 68IN.
(A tapestry was made for The Marquis of Bute
from this painting by the Edinburgh Tapestry Co.)

The Queen's Street Café with Dr Thomson, 1989,
oil on canvas, 173 × 152.5CM, 68 × 60IN.
(Scottish National Portrait Gallery)

Anya, 1985,
oil on canvas, 152.5 × 152.5CM, 60 × 60IN.
(Courtesy The National Portrait Gallery, London)

Paul, 1982,
oil on canvas, 172.5 × 122CM, 68 × 48IN.

The Presentation of Time (Homage to Rubens), 1987, oil on canvas (diptych), 244 × 345CM, 96 × 135¾IN.

A Long Night's Journey into Day, 1987, oil on canvas (diptych), 243.8 × 345.4CM, 97½ × 138IN

Self-Portrait (Chez Moi), 1987, oil on canvas, 213.5 × 274CM, 84 × 108IN.

The Screeching Gannet, 1987, oil on canvas, 173 × 173CM, 68 × 68IN.
(The Metropolitan Museum of Art, purchase)
Roy R. and Marie S. Neuberger gift, 1988

Self-Portrait, 1988,
oil on canvas, 121.5 × 91.5CM,
48 × 36IN.

Self-Portrait, 1988,
oil on canvas, 121.5 × 91.5CM,
48 × 36IN.

The Patient II, 1988, oil on canvas, 173 × 152.5CM, 68 × 60IN.
(Collection Susan Kasen Summer and Robert D. Summer)

Self-Portrait in Hospital I, 1988, etching (edition of 20), paper size 63 × 56CM, 25 × 22IN.

Self-Portrait in Hospital II, 1988,
etching (edition of 20),
paper size 63 × 56CM, 24¾ × 22IN.

The Transplant I, 1989,
etching (edition of 30),
paper size 56 × 63CM, 22 × 24¾IN.

London Scene, 1989, oil on canvas, 152.5 × 172.5CM, 60 × 68IN.

Prometheus III, 1989, oil on canvas, 213.5 × 185CM, 84 × 72¾IN.

CHAPTER 8

Plumbing the Depths

If any proof were needed to illustrate the rise in Bellany's fortunes, it came when the Earl of Gowrie, on the day he was appointed Minister for Arts following Margaret Thatcher's second election victory, sent his official car round to Windmill Drive to collect Bellany paintings to hang in his office. That same year, 1983, Bellany was commissioned by the Scottish National Portrait Gallery to paint a portrait of himself and Alan Davie. 'Just as Bellany's paintings have inspired a younger generation of Scottish artists, so did Davie's before that inspire Bellany's generation. This double portrait is the homage of one artist to another,' reads the caption. Bellany had come a long way from those days twenty years before when he dreamed of glory on the Port Seton bus.

Monika Kinley secured Bellany's most important exhibition to date, a one-man touring exhibition starting at the Ikon Gallery, Birmingham, and finishing the following year. 'Somewhere beyond the implacable, silent images in a Bellany painting the sound of ancestral voices can be heard from a distant and deceptive antiquity,' began Victor Musgrave, English champion of Outsider Art, the art of individual compulsion, in his catalogue tribute.[29] On the day of the press launch I remember Bellany handing round the Bacardi miniatures before the train had pulled out of Euston; and later leading a successful raid on the office of the director of the Birmingham art gallery, persuading him to open his drink-drawer 'in office hours'.

His private life was falling apart but you would never have known it from his jovial behaviour. Monika Kinley and Victor Musgrave both fell ill, Juliet was in hospital most of the time and he had virtually stopped eating as he suffered the first symptoms of liver failure. 'He let me feel it once and it was rock solid,' recalls Bert Irvin. His ankles swelled from water retention and he intermittently passed blood as a result of minor haemorrhages. Helen came to his rescue when things came to a head on Anya's fourteenth birthday in September 1984. 'Juliet was in hospital and John was on his own,' recalls Helen. 'He was on top form, however, and suggested that in celebration of the birthday we should go to Dieppe.

This was where we'd gone on honeymoon and it was always special but I really felt I should keep my distance and not get involved in any sentimental journey. However, he pleaded with us and so next morning we found ourselves on the early ferry from Newhaven. As Anya said, "That's something I've always liked about Dad, doing things on the spur of the moment." Again he was in great form, cracking jokes and telling stories, accompanied as usual by the hip-flask. In the clear morning light I suddenly became aware that he was bright yellow. He also wanted to tell me about various "allergies" he thought he had. I was panic-stricken. If my suspicions were correct we were on a journey that for him might have no return.

'We had taken my car and on arrival in France he insisted that we drive around the coast. Quite by accident we came across the churchyard at Varangeville where Braque is buried. We visited the tiny church and stood in homage at the grave. We had nothing to offer until John suddenly remembered he had a postcard of one of his own paintings in his pocket. He placed it on the gravestone and we left to look for somewhere to have lunch. The children were laughing, everyone was drawing as we went along and John was wound up with delight at the jaunt. "C'est bien ici" he found time to write on a postcard to Monika Kinley. It was a respite from the misery surrounding him. He was irrepressible. "I just don't want this day to end," he told us.

'When I got back to London I called the doctor. I warned John that this time he could not shout me down. He would be going to hospital whether he liked it or not and, furthermore, this would be the parting of the ways for him and his best friend, the booze. To my surprise he put up no fight and almost seemed relieved. From that day to this he has not touched alcohol.'

John Bellany with one of his paintings in the garden of his parents' house in Port Seton

Scottish Fish Gutter, 8 × 6ft, laid out prior to framing

Dear John [*wrote John Bratby that October*], heard from Gus you've been in St Thomas's, from work and whiskey. I drink too much & am afeard of it – Terrified.

6 days ago me 'and shook so much when I peed my cock was here there and everywhere. I daresay you do not care to hear about that. Anyway thought I'd drop you a line. Did not like to hear of you falling by the wayside. Still we are not indestructible. Look at ol' Richard Burton: the drink killed him indirectly: broke him. Its a terrible thing drink, & yet such a good companion.

Thank you so much for phoning about the Arkwright Centre Show, & the Birthday Song.

Take it easy (fatuous advice)

Regards John.

John Bellany at Braque's grave

Just as traumatic was 1985. His father and Juliet both died but Bellany shared first prize with Paul Huxley

Allegory laid out in the garden of his parents' house, prior to framing

With Monika Kinley and Tony Kirk at the first New York exhibition, Rosa Esman Gallery

to win the first Athena Art Award, at £25,000 the most valuable art prize in Britain. As an abstract painter Huxley welcomed the judges' decision to reward Bellany: 'Probably because he has what I don't have, a gusto for expressing emotional states. Everything comes out – nightmares, joy, exuberance. He is an extraordinarily fluent painter whereas I am very slow; and I envy him coming from where he does. I was born in a London suburb, which I liked, but his background gives his art a wonderfully salty, gutsy character.'

Plans were already afoot for Bellany's major retrospective at the National Gallery of Modern Art in 1986. With Monika Kinley and Keith Hartley, he visited Port Seton that summer to look at some of his early paintings, which were then still stored in his father's garage. 'I'll never forget the sight of those treasures,' says Monika Kinley. They laid them out on the grass in the little back garden.

Robin Gibson had also approached him to paint a series of portraits for an exhibition at the National Portrait Gallery, which Bellany now proceeded to do with his usual energy, despite his weakened physical state. 'Even by the standards of a full-time portrait painter, John Bellany's work in this field over the past eighteen months or so would rank as prodigious,' wrote Gibson in the catalogue foreword in 1986.[30]

In October Bellany visited Cheshire to fulfil an official commission from the gallery to paint a portrait of Ian Botham, the first cricketer to be honoured in this way since W.G. Grace. The painting would be the centrepiece of the National Portrait Gallery show. Because Botham had little time to spare, Bellany, despite his ill-health, had to risk the long journey north to do the portrait in the house of Botham's manager, Tim Hudson. It proved one of the most lucrative moves of his career.

The house was a Queen Anne mansion for which Hudson was building a private cricket ground surrounded by a fence in his club colours of red, green and yellow; in fact, he and his wife Maxi were such exuberant people they outshone the illustrious sportsman. But Botham too was a magnificent specimen, a physical giant of a man whom Bellany found an intriguing subject. 'I never talk when I begin painting,' he says, 'but later, when the sitter's getting tired, I encourage it. Botham said the way I painted reminded him of bowling. He would study a batsman with the same intensity, looking for their strengths and weaknesses, and then lull them into a state of false security before delivering a killer ball.'

Hudson was so pleased with the Botham portrait that he commissioned Bellany to paint portraits of him, his wife, his daughter River, his Uncle Charlie and the West Indian cricket captain Viv Richards; and he bought, sight unseen, the entire Portrait Gallery show (except for the unavailable Botham portrait). By any standards it was a dashing gesture of patronage.

The year was crowned by his signing terms with one of the most prestigious international galleries and certainly the foremost in London in terms of German Expressionism, Fischer Fine Art. It is symptomatic of his relative anonymity in London even at this date that Wolfgang and Jutta Fischer had not heard of him. Mary Rose Beaumont made the introduction and they were overwhelmed, both by the 'wild gestural' painting he was currently doing and the 'mythological Celtic' pictures from the 1960s which he was understandably reluctant to reveal, having very few left. 'And of course he's also a great draughtsman,' says Jutta Fischer. They offered terms immediately. Bellany had to leave Monika Kinley, an unhappy incident; Victor Musgrave, her long-time associate, died soon after. She still carries on the work of the Outsider Archive in his memory.

In this difficult and tragic time Bellany's chief solace was Helen and his rediscovered love for her. Like a harbour regained, a calm settled on his art, which he produced as abundantly as ever: *La Vie en Rose* (1985), *My Grandfather* (1985), *Comment Ça Va* (1985) and *Celtic Lovebirds* (1985), all done in a spirit of gentle acceptance – clear, uncluttered and resigned.

The family at John Bellany's retrospective exhibition at the Scottish National Gallery of Modern Art, Edinburgh, 1986

'John Bellany: New Portraits', consisting of twelve oil paintings and seven watercolours and drawings completed in 1985, was exhibited at the National Portrait Gallery from February to May 1986. What he had encouraged with his prize-winning entry for the NPG's Imperial Tobacco Portrait Award in 1980 now came to fruition: 'The old policy had been to act as a "postage stamp" collection of pictures of famous faces, but after 1980 they accepted paintings for the first time.' In other words, the merit of the pictures as an example of an artist's work was as important a criterion as its subject. As Gibson wrote: 'Portraits by a basically romantic artist of our time such as John Bellany are not passports for instant recognition and admittance into a given social and cultural milieu but personal statements by the artist about himself and his friends, and a re-creation in his own pictorial terms of his ideas and reactions to the subject.'[31]

Not everyone agreed. The unveiling of the Botham portrait caused more press coverage than the rest of Bellany's career put together, proving one of the most contentious contemporary acquisitions by a public gallery in post-1945 Britain. It gathered numerous hostile headlines – from 'Art lovers hit portrait for six' to 'Howzat, Botham' – and the ultimate accolade of the odd cartoon, 'Peter Simple' in the *Daily Telegraph* had a field day. 'John Bellany' – his surname was widely misspelt – 'painter of a remarkable portrait of Ian Botham in the National Portrait Gallery which shows the great man with a small, almost epicene head on a very large body, says: "I wanted to capture Ian's presence, both physical and spiritual, the aura he commands when he steps on to the cricket field and the crowd trembles."

'Mr Bellamy [sic] is not the only artist who has sought to capture the titanic cricketer's physical

Helen and John Bellany's second
wedding, 1986

*Helen, c.*1987,
oil on canvas, 122 × 91.5CM,
48 × 36IN.

and spiritual presence. John Gasby, the neo-explosionist sculptor, has produced, after months of dedicated work, a statue of Botham, several times life size, which he hopes will be erected outside Lord's, involving the diversion of several roads.'[32]

Bellany's commissioned portraits are, by his own reckoning, a minor aspect of his work, and the Botham portrait is far from his best. It is not a good facial likeness but it is demonstrably a 'Bellany' and it does convey the man's aura of sporting invincibility as one of the great all-rounders in cricket history. As Betty Irvin comments: 'John may not capture a photographic likeness but he always gets something.'

In 1986 John and Helen were remarried with only their children present: 'It was magic,' says Jonathan, 'as a kid that was all we'd ever wished.' They moved to another house on the edge of Clapham Common.

Bellany's health continued to deteriorate and his career to prosper. The major retrospective exhibition 'John Bellany: Paintings, Watercolours and Drawings 1964–1986' duly took place at the new Scottish National Gallery of Modern Art during the Edinburgh Festival. There was a handsome catalogue with essays by Sandy Moffat and Alan Bold, who also wrote a poem, 'The Voyage of John Bellany: A Triptych', and an introduction and extended picture captions by Keith Hartley, assistant keeper. A thirty-minute film by Keith Alexander, *John Bellany,* and a fifteen-minute film by Joan Bakewell, *John Bellany – The Making of a Portrait,* both for BBC Television, were screened on both sides of the border. In London the exhibition was shown at the Serpentine Gallery, under the directorship of Alister Warman, to coincide with a show of the artist's new work which was chosen to supplement an exhibition by Bryan Kneale to inaugurate the Henry Moore Gallery in the Royal College of Art.

The films show an invalid, hollow-eyed and shallow-breathed but bravely making light of it. 'I got a bit of a fright,' he tells Keith Alexander, 'so I've had to quell my passions in a certain direction, which is much better. So I'm just happy as anything living a full life again. I'm fine now, as you can see.'

In reality he could only eat liquidised food; and calories – sweets, Coca-Cola – not protein, not even a slice of bread. Apart from suffering agonising toothache, he was prevented from sleeping by an intolerable itching; so intolerable he would invariably have five baths in the course of a night. 'I couldn't eat, I couldn't sleep and I had this permanent rash all over me. I had this special oil to put in the bath but after five minutes I'd be itching worse than ever. Obviously the liver was collapsing, so the whole system was starting to go wrong. I would get frights. In fact, my nerve ends were totally frayed, so I was completely on edge. It was a living hell. Of course, it must have been absolutely terrible for everyone else, especially for Helen and the children. The other thing is I was literally fading away. I was starting to look like somebody who was already dead. When I see the photographs now I nearly collapse. I look like someone out of Buchenwald.'

Apart from sudden haemorrhages – one, in particular, was nearly fatal – he also suffered fits of delirium and delusion, when he was deprived of logic or memory and could be a dangerous liability, a hazard with fire, gas or water. Helen was exhausted from constant vigilance. In addition, congestion made his breathing increasingly difficult. Long gone was the sight of him – a happy memory of only three years before – dancing a jig while simultaneously playing the accordion. Now he was frail and swathed in sweaters, and walked with the help of a stick. How he painted at all in such circumstances was a triumph of the will; to paint so tenderly a mark of noble character. *Self-Portrait* (1987), measuring nine-and-a-half by seven feet, the largest work from this period, is a triumph of mind over matter. It centres on the small detail of the watch dangling from his hand. Time was indeed in his hands: 'I was on that edge of life and death for about a year and it was getting closer and closer.'

The only thing that kept him going on his frequent spells in St Thomas's was being able to paint and draw. 'One wonderful thing about St Thomas's was that it has one of the best views in the world up or down the Thames depending what ward I was on – they always made sure I was near a window. They should think of the view when they build hospitals; it's very important to people's recovery. They were incredibly kind; and because I couldn't sleep they let me work during the night. I was always in the ward for no-hopers and everybody round about me was dying. It always seemed to be in the bed next to me or directly opposite! Some guy I'd been speaking to just hours before; so I was always in the presence of death. It's so easy to die, just to go – no question of that. But I didn't want to die. My mind was alert. There was still so much to say, so much to live for and life was so precious and that's what kept me going.'

He managed to keep painting, and did some tumultuous bird's-eye views of the Thames in the tradition of Kokoschka, one of which, the best in his opinion, he gave to the hospital. Meanwhile, his recognition as an artist continued to grow. In 1986 there was the retrospective at the National Gallery of Modern Art; the broadcast of Keith Alexander's thirty-minute documentary film for BBC Television; and a major commission from the Marquess of Bute for a tapestry of Bellany's painting of *Janus*, the two-headed god of all beginning (from which we derive the word January), which was woven at the Bute-owned Dovecote Studio.

The exhibitions proliferated: in 1987 in Australia, in 1988 in New York and the Hamburg Kunsthalle, on the invitation of the director, Werner Hofmann. It was the first retrospective exhibition by a British artist in a German museum since the war. Somehow he managed to attend both 1988 shows although, as Helen says, 'he could have died any minute'. Nevertheless, for most of the period from 1986 to 1988 he was in and out of hospital.

'John is and always has been seriously phobic about death. His own approaching death he could never have contemplated and so it was a lonely and dreadful secret to have to keep,' remembers Helen. 'I was advised to try and share the burden by gently broaching the subject with him if an opportunity arose. It never did. It never would have.

'The decline accelerated over four years and the dreaded moment of truth came a few days before Christmas in 1987 when the consultants at St Thomas's gathered round his bed. So many times their skill had saved him but this time the game was up. "We can do no more to help you and there isn't much time left," they said. I froze on the spot as he shouted out: "But I want to live as long as Picasso." He meant it. He was in despair.

'I found myself asking: "What about a transplant?" And was shocked to hear myself voice a previously unconsidered option. It must have been panic, and in retrospect I wonder which had horrified John more, death or a transplant – about equal, I should say. In 1988 liver transplants were still considered by many to be experimental. We certainly knew nothing about them, nothing positive anyway. Four months later as I saw John down to the operating theatre in Addenbrooke's Hospital we were still of the impression that if he survived he might have a few extra months at best.'

An interview was arranged at King's College Hospital, Dulwich, where he was told that to prove his suitability for a transplant he would have to undergo a series of tests. Compared with the spanking new St Thomas's with its views over the Thames, King's College was grim, despite the kindness of the nurses. Nor were things improved by the flippant welcome of the consultant: 'I was looking at *The Times* on Saturday and saw that a John Bellany of Clapham had died; so I'm rather surprised to see you here today.' It made things no better when he tried to correct himself by adding: 'So many of the patients on the waiting list die before a suitable organ becomes available.'

Helen recalls: 'We returned home to spend several more weeks making frantic, usually dead-of-night dashes to St Thomas's and in between times holding our breath and waiting. In spite of our anxiety, and in all humility, we were mindful that in order for John to be given this final chance, the ultimate sacrifice of a precious life would have to be offered.'

It did not prevent him embarking on a series of large, eight-by-six-foot paintings of himself in St Thomas's, his bed surrounded by various groups of visitors. He also decided to paint five-by-four-foot portraits of the children and Helen in various combinations, alone and together. The colour is bleached, the figures half-realised, an unconscious distancing and disintegration. *A Paix* (1986) does not just have a yearning title but is suffused with a cold, North Sea light.

In a last feverish burst he summoned 'the energy of a twenty-one-year-old' to paint farewell paintings, thank you paintings, tribute paintings and others more agonisingly self-questioning, 'pretty gruesome ones', notably a series on Prometheus, a symbol of perpetual torture, whose liver was consumed by a vulture through the day and restored at night. *Prometheus II* (1988) is a frantic image of survival, a half-dead, half-alive figure with a gaping wound in its side and flailing matchstick arms.

After further lobbying by Helen they heard that Addenbrooke's Hospital was willing to take Bellany as a patient. A date was finalised for him to go to Cambridge to undergo a further set of tests in the spring of 1988.

'It was the Friday and we were to go up on the Monday. He was so weak I was at my wits' end wondering how to keep him alive.' They drove down to visit their old friends Gus and Angie Cummins. 'Afterwards, we had to walk up a steep hill from the house to get back to the car. It was bitter and John was shivering so much Gus gave him his coat. But John couldn't find his breath after a while and had to rest several times. Somehow we got him back to the car. "Oh, that was a near thing," he said with relief. I saw Gus had tears in his eyes.'

The tests at Dulwich proved to be only preliminary, 'a qualification for the Olympics', as Bellany put it. Helen compared this second ordeal with the exams he had sat long ago for the Royal College of Art; only now the verdict was life or death. There were sometimes as many as half a dozen tests a day over a period of a week. One, he remembers, involved cycling upside-down, a particularly strenuous version of running on the spot. There was competition from other patients who had come from all over the world; and always there was the spectre of failure, of being told, as several of his fellow examinees were, that there was no chance. But Bellany continued drawing, portraits of patients and the staff, whom he liked immensely.

'That was unbelievable. Addenbrooke's for me is the best hospital in the universe. They were so friendly, so reassuring. They were uplifting. They gave you verve, the staff-nurse and the doctor in charge. What a lift! Funny – afterwards they said: "Whenever we saw you coming through the door we said: 'He'll not die!'" Because they always can tell, they can tell from the eyes if the person's got the spirit, the will. And I had that determined look about me. There was laughter and humour, as well, that was another thing.'

Helen confirms the difference this made: 'Everyone was so optimistic. "We'll soon sort you out!" was the attitude.'

The tests were successful but that was not the end of the waiting. He now joined a queue for a donor. The liver not only had to match his particular bio-chemical pattern but the organs themselves were difficult to obtain as storage had not yet been developed. This was perhaps the most taxing time of all.

'Early on the Friday evening the Scottish doctor I had been drawing came back and drew the screens around, so I thought something dreadful was going to happen. And she said: "I've got to talk to you very quickly. You're not top of the queue but we've got a liver that fits you and not the people above you. So do you want to go through with the transplant? – because the liver's in the helicopter now, being delivered, and we'll have to operate immediately. You know the risks." And I said: "I think I do but you'd better tell me again." So she said: "Of every three that go in two come out alive." So I said: "Yes, I'll go for it; but on one condition. You'll have to come back to let me finish the portrait, because it may be the last I'll ever do." So she said: "I'll do that with the greatest pleasure," and she did.'

Dr Kim Jacobson remembers it differently: 'Next morning when we went down for the anaesthetic he said, "Look on the desk" – he'd spent most of the night painting to have it ready for me.'[33]

'After the painting was finished I got mentally prepared,' says Bellany. 'It was the longest operation in the world then – eight hours – and I knew there was no point going into it petrified. I had to give it 110 per cent or I'd not survive, because it needed all my strength; so I had to build up all the power and faith and energy and love and hope to get myself ready.'

Bellany was still joking as Helen accompanied him down to the operating theatre. It was 6 a.m. on 30 April – tomorrow would be May Day, the seaman's distress call, an irony not lost on him.

John Bellany, two weeks before his liver transplant operation, April 1988

Death Knell for John Knox, 1990, watercolour, 76 × 57CM, 30 × 22IN.

With Sarah Webb (daughter of King Webb), a friend and neighbour, Eversden, 1989

CHAPTER 9

Relaunched

Bellany knew he had survived when he saw a nurse standing beside him but he did not believe it until he touched her. He was masked so he had to signal for a piece of paper on which he wrote: 'Can I draw you?' She nodded and he made the first drawing of his new life, hardly legible, like the trembling line of a seismograph. Almost illegibly he annotated it: 'I will live. I will be OK.' This was the first day after his operation. He did not draw again until he left intensive care.

'The day he came out of the intensive care ward,' remembers Sir Roy Calne, the pioneering surgeon of liver transplantation, 'he asked not for analgesics but paper and pen. I've never come across anybody who the day they came out of the intensive care ward started resuming their profession.' And this a man whose liver had been the worst Calne had seen in six hundred transplant operations. How Bellany had stayed alive before the operation was a mystery, and his equally remarkable recovery can be explained only by the will to live fuelled by his desire to make art.

For him drawing was an analgesic. The pain was indescribable but 'as soon as the tip of the pencil touched the paper I no longer felt it'. The concentration required of drawing and painting had similarly dispelled his terror before the operation, momentarily but completely occupying his mind.

He covered the glacial blue walls of his room (do hospitals consider the psychological effects of colour? Blue is deathly but yellow symbolises sunny good health) with posters, postcards and, in time, his own drawings and watercolours; anything for colour. In pride of place was the illustrated invitation card for his latest exhibition at Reg Singh's Beaux Arts Gallery in Bath, showing an image of the Ancient Mariner.

Most of the watercolours and drawings were self-portraits and are a remarkable testimony to his own resilience and the progress of a patient recovering from major surgery. This progress was disrupted by an infection which made the dreaded rejection of the transplanted liver a nerve-wracking possibility and put him back briefly in intensive care. But he survived; and his drawing traces that slow ordeal with an unblinking, raw and deeply moving honesty. That favourite compliment of his, an art that 'plumbed the depths', was never more applicable.

As usual, the view from his window was important. At Addenbrooke's he could see over the Cambridge countryside. 'May's a great time of year for anyone to have an operation because the whole of nature's in sympathy: "Come on! Cheer up! Get better!" it says. There was a sunny Sunday morning when I could hear this brass band and hymn-singing from miles away, and I just couldn't stop the tears. I cried a lot after the operation; all the pent-up emotion. And listening to that music I thought: "This is a good omen".'

He found music, the more romantic the better, his chief solace after drawing, and dates his love of Sibelius in particular from those first days. There were times when he had such insights into musical meaning that he thought the stranger to whom he owed his life must have been a composer!

Already by 12 May he was well enough to receive visitors. Bert and Betty Irvin were the first. Bert Irvin recorded his impressions in his diary: 'John was in his single room in Ward C9 with balloons tied to his bedhead. Watercolours & drawings that he's done since he's been there were on the walls, as was the photograph of himself & Helen by Lord Snowdon, & several of his postcards. The rest were in a box under the bed. He looked yellow and his eyes were very yellow, as Helen had warned us.

'He was magnificent. His will to survive and optimism were indomitable. His sense of humour was superbly and ridiculously intact, as when he insisted we have photographs taken with him with his pyjamas open & his operation & pipes & bags & bottles on display.'

Letters, telephone calls and visits from friends were a great source of encouragement. Messages of goodwill came from old friends in Port Seton, from the art world and from his collectors and sitters. Frequent telephone calls from Sean Connery in Spain and David Bowie in California, the latter a keen collector of his work, were the talk of the hospital. He was now a celebrity among celebrities.

One day he drew a self-portrait that especially pleased him by the way 'it had drawn itself'. He was admiring it when his doctors came round. 'How are you?' they asked; and he pointed to the drawing. 'Do not go gentle into that good night. Rage, rage against the dying of the light,' he said, quoting Dylan Thomas. 'Anyone who could do that is bound to live.' His audience broke into spontaneous applause.

With the rapid improvement in his health he was given the choice of convalescing near Cambridge or returning to London. He chose Cambridge and the countryside, and by the first week in June had made such progress that he was able to leave the hospital at weekends to be nursed by Helen in the cottage she had rented in the nearby village of Eversden while he was in hospital. 'I was the luckiest guy in the universe. Everything got better, even my hearing. Where I had been like a wilting flower suddenly I was blossoming. It was as if I'd drunk the elixir of life. My skin, the strength in my hands, my hair – I was

With Bert Irving and Helen ten days after the liver transplant operation. An infection turned him deep yellow and caused him to suffer great pain

twenty-five again! And of course it affected my painting.' He still (1994) does not need spectacles.

Sitting out in the garden he saw the birds and flowers with new eyes. In particular a black, crimson and white greater spotted woodpecker came within a few feet, as if welcoming him home. He painted a celebratory self-portrait in party gear of tuxedo and bow-tie. 'I think that man in the painting's demanding an exit permit,' he told Roy Calne. Calne agreed. Bellany was discharged, subject to fortnightly check-ups which, by 1994, had become half-yearly. Roy and Patsy Calne are now among the Bellanys' closest friends.

His first outing was to have dinner with neighbours Joan Bakewell and Jack Emery; an evening made memorable by eating in the garden to the sound of Berlioz's *Te Deum* echoing from the house. 'I was alive and among friends – what a feeling!'

On their first visit to the cottage Bert and Betty Irvin were amused to find one room stacked solid with stretched canvases. Soon the artist was indeed strong enough to embark on oil paintings, starting with small three-by-fours and working up to six-footers, many of them of flowers. 'I was still doing self-portraits but the beauty of flowers . . . they were so life-giving.' He returned to the legend of Prometheus: 'I was surprised how I could keep painting when I was dying, but it amazed me even more how quickly I was able to pick it up again after the operation.'

He was tackling large canvases within two months. This feat should not be underestimated: a fully fit friend of the author's who took up painting at the age of fifty soon abandoned the idea because his legs and arms could not take the strain. Painting is manual labour.

Nothing illustrated the speed of Bellany's recovery more dramatically than the permission he received to attend the artists' night of the 'Late Picasso' exhibition at the Tate. His stitches were still intact and he was only able to stay a short time, but it was just the tonic he needed. He also enjoyed going for drives, while the friendliness of his neighbours made Eversden 'a second Port Seton'. Gradually, too, through his Addenbrooke's contacts, he became involved in university life, a process which culminated in his being elected Fellow Commoner of Trinity Hall in 1990.

He also pleasingly settled some unfinished business: a portfolio of etchings of Hemingway's *Old Man and the Sea* for Charles Booth Clibborn started in St Thomas's. Printed by the Peacock Press in Aberdeen, it joined his other etchings in the collection of the Museum of Modern Art. It was also bought by the Hemingway Library at Harvard, where it is on permanent display.

In 1989 he was commissioned by Dr Fitzhugh, publicity director of London Underground, to paint a picture as the first of a new series of posters advertising the tube stations. The painting, *Chinatown*, was for Piccadilly Circus, adjacent to the Chinatown district of Soho. The poster was so popular that he was commissioned to paint another, *Camden Lock*, advertising Chalk Farm. Both continue to be in circulation.

When Bellany was strong enough the family returned to their London house on the north side of Clapham Common, where he resumed painting in only slightly less cramped conditions than the cottage. Luck now intervened once more when a notice of sale for their old and much-loved house at Windmill Drive arrived in the post. Bellany hurried over and immediately decided to buy. Apart from sentimental reasons, the ground-floor and basement had been converted into one huge open-plan space, ideal for a studio.

He was now able to paint large canvases without inconvenience and found that the space, particularly the view afforded by a minstrel's gallery, enabled him to step away from the work and see it with 'a fresh eye'. It was 1989: 'The fire in the belly was back, the vigour was back, things were going well.' The colour that had faded from his paintings before the operation, he now realises, returned with a vengeance. 'Colour has flooded back,' said Sandy Moffat, 'like blood surging back into the body of the paintings.'[34] Instead of pallor there were deep yellows, deep carmine red. He had cheated the 'Old Man'. He was jubilant. 'I felt like Ben Gunn. I could even eat cheese again!' For Jutta Fischer, his returning powers were displayed in another way: 'What John began to get back was the gesture; and that's gone from strength to strength.'

A year after the operation he was back at Addenbrooke's in the same theatre, drawing a liver transplant. The recipient was a boy of eight and the medical team was the same one that had operated on him. The little boy's life was saved to the sound of Mozart's *Magic Flute*. It was one of the most moving experiences of his life and he was astonished by what he saw: 'Just the skill of these people, standing up all that time, working with that intensity. The stitching! I couldn't believe the speed of it, like someone drawing frenetically. How they can do it day after day, week after week. These people are underrated. So many bad things happen – let's hear sometimes about some of the great things that happen.' The drawings acted as preparatory studies for a suite of etchings. The boy's health has flourished.

Important shows in 1989 exhibited the graphic work recording his miraculous recovery; 'The Renaissance of John Bellany: Watercolours painted in Addenbrooke's Hospital, Cambridge' and 'John Bellany: a Renaissance' both toured after being launched at the Scottish National Gallery of Modern Art, Edinburgh. In some of this work there is an understandable sentimentality and a bias towards illustrative documentation but Norman Reid, for one, found it marked a new departure. 'I thought he was too close to Beckmann for comfort in the earlier work; and I was delighted to find in these new works so much more of himself.' He also found the watercolours a revelation.

Bellany's association with Fischer Fine Art meant his work was properly exposed at international art fairs for the first time; in 1990 there was a moment when he had independent one-man shows simultaneously in New York, Berlin and Glasgow.

He and Helen divided their time between periods of urban stimulus and rural hibernation. Having bought Windmill Drive, they now began to look for something permanent near Cambridge. Eventually they found what they wanted, a converted late-seventeenth-century clock-house. Not only did they enjoy the seclusion of being surrounded by a huge garden at the centre of Capability Brown parkland, but the ground-floor room, which spanned the width of the building, made another, ideal, light-filled studio.

Each of these studios is fully equipped, even to the table piled with a mound of guano-like paint which he uses as a palette. It enables him to travel light and to work as soon as he arrives. He has found the spacious new circumstances of his life a release: 'Having room to hang things and stack them – actually to let them breathe – has helped enormously.'

In Scotland the painter had been most eloquently championed critically by Sandy Moffat and Alan Bold. Their insight afforded by close friendship over thirty years leaves them unmatched; but in the 1980s he found a new and conspicuously zealous champion south of the border in Peter Fuller, best remembered as the founding editor of the magazine *Modern Painters*. The magazine owed its Ruskinian title to Fuller's conversion to painting which he considered to have spiritual value – even, one feels, had he been able to overcome his agnosticism – Christian value. And in Bellany, after initially dismissing his most torrid work of the early 1980s as an 'indulgent *mélange*', he found a painter worthy of symbolising his ideal.

The two became friends and in 1990 Bellany invited Fuller to write the catalogue introduction to his exhibitions at the Compass Gallery in Glasgow and Raab Gallery in Berlin. 'At forty-eight,' declared Fuller, 'John Bellany is emerging as unquestionably the most outstanding British painter of his generation: that, at least, is the conclusion I have reached after seeing the remarkable works which he has been producing since the death of his mother in 1989.'[35]

Tragically, Fuller was killed in a car crash only weeks after these words were written. He had agreed to write the equivalent of this book, the first monograph, and had sat for his portrait at Windmill Drive the day before the accident. Snowdon's memorable photograph of Bellany bearing the symbolic burden of a huge haddock on his back – a photographic evocation of his first etching, *The Burden* – was taken the week after Fuller's death and bears poignant witness to that shocking loss.[36]

Proximity to Cambridge meant he could continue his treatment at Addenbrooke's as well as consolidating his links with the university. He became close friends with Colin Renfrew, professor of archaeology and Master of Jesus College, and his wife Jane, vice-president of Lucy Cavendish College. His pride in his Fellowship and delight in these and other academic friendships is obvious but he is still aware that even at the highest intellectual level visual erudition is not respected in England. 'They say communication is about talking, talking; but for me it's about looking, looking. People feel free to dismiss art in the most ludicrous terms; and yet I, as an artist, would not dream of commenting on Beckett without first reading Dostoevsky and the Bible.'

In 1991 the retiring director of the Fizwilliam Museum, Michael Jaffe, and his successor, Michael Jervis, jointly invited him to exhibit his new work. His painting *Sarah Webb: Daughter of King Webb*, their next-door neighbour in Eversden, was subsequently also bought for the permanent collection.

There were other significant public purchases in Britain and abroad, by the Scottish National Gallery of Modern Art, Glasgow Museums and the Metropolitan Museum of Art, New York, which bought *The Screaming Gannet*. His work also entered museums in Europe and Australia and some notable private collections, not least that of the Americans Bob Summer and Susan Kasen Summer with the result of another firm friendship. The continuing improvement of his health and the end of the Bellanys' financial worries meant they could travel for the first time when and where they liked. He now roamed farther afield – most excitingly, for him, to Italy for the first time, where they lived for some months, and Spain.

In his introduction to the catalogue for Bellany's retrospective at the Kelvingrove Art Gallery and Museum, in Glasgow in 1992, Sandy Moffat wrote: 'The year 1990 marked the beginning of a rich new period in Bellany's painting. Since then, or so it seems to me, Bellany has returned to full power as an artist.'[37] The show was limited to paintings only from the periods 1971–72 and 1991–92, which not only revealed the remarkable levels of his output but also the difference in mood. Black in the earlier period 'when I had a crow on my shoulder', and predominantly from the warm, red end of the spectrum in the new work. In the earlier paintings there is a powerful sense of existential isolation, with solitary, victimised figures; the later work, in contrast, teems with people and detail, sometimes to the point of figurative marmalade. But in the frenetic *Lovers* (1991), the old power is back and the paint once again gets the better of line.

His children all agree that he has calmed down a lot as a person since the operation but not in his art. As Paul says: 'Most people never get a chance to stop and weigh up their life. However, I don't think he's mellowed in his art.'

'As you get older you think: "Painting's just about feeling". Rembrandt, Van Gogh – that's what

With his daughter, Anya,
Cambridge, 1992

they're all about,' Bellany remarked, while selecting the illustrations for this book. This is overwhelmingly true of *Sunset Song*, painted in 1991 in commemoration of his mother's death two years before. Driving back from Eyemouth on the day of the funeral he had witnessed a superb sunset which he incorporates into this torrid threnody.

The British Council arranged for him to tour several key cities in Eastern Europe as a roving artist-in-residence. For six months in 1993 he and Helen visited Vienna, Prague and Budapest. They drove extensively, meeting as many people and absorbing as much as they could. Bellany did pencil or watercolour sketches, regularly returning to England to complete what has become a series of monumental paintings on the most epic European subject of his lifetime, the collapse of the Russian Empire and, with it, the end of communism as a ruling economic force in Eastern Europe. What he discovered was disconcertingly familiar. Here were tens of thousands of lost souls in the form of a titanic wave of refugees; here were golden calves on every street corner, as the crudest market-forces prevailed. Here was the Danube, as symbolic of hope as the River Jordan, which connects the painting as it connects the three ancient cities, underlying the theme of human migration, of minds and lives in flux.

Each city is roughly defined in the pictures by a characteristic subject; for Budapest it is the refugees; for Prague, the prostitutes; for Vienna, the fortune-tellers. *The Sword Swallower* plied his desperate trade outside a café in Budapest and is a powerful metaphor for the political division of the Czechs and Slovaks, which happened during Bellany's stay. The division of the state seemed no less horrifying a risk. In the painting one hand is described in detail while the other is virtually non-existent, deliberately 'let go like the country itself'.

Prague Easter depicts Easter Monday morning on Charles Bridge. This again alludes to the separation they experienced, evoking the feverish sense of activity and uncertainty that Easter weekend. 'Easter's always a haunting time anyway and to be on this bridge with the crucifixion in the middle of it and all these anxious people, many of them looking utterly dejected, was an eerie experience.'

Seeing so many displaced and stricken people living by their wits on a pittance by normal European standards was profoundly distressing – particularly the beautiful young girls reduced to prostitution, and the old ladies in the flea-market selling their heirlooms to stay alive. But he was impressed by their intrepid spirit and religious faith which had survived half a century of communist repression, represented on the one hand by *Goodnight Vienna* and on the other by *Old Woman at Prayer*.

This new subject matter did not stop him painting pictures on familiar themes, in fact it seems even to have sharpened his appetite. *Jock Dickson's* draws on the memory of his fish-gutting days which enriched his life and art to such a degree. The observation of the preoccupied boy on the right and the three watchful women is both tender and precise; the mood informs the colour; the painting of the fish in the tray is a bravura still-life in itself. It is for these spontaneous portraits, his self-portraits especially, that he will surely be remembered as a portraitist, rather than the commissions of the great and good.

Sabbath Ennui recalls the discount side of childhood in a small place where everyone knew everyone else's business, 'the net-curtain syndrome' as he calls it. 'I can remember sitting at Sunday dinner in my Sunday best aware that there were things going on but still too young to understand. I like the white tablecloth and the hidden presences.' It is a picture only made positive with the hindsight of age, when distance lends objectivity and, among those one has loved, the dead begin to outnumber the living.

John Bellany photographed by
Lord Snowdon

Ancestors, 1990, oil on canvas, 213 × 218.5CM, 80 × 86IN.
(Collection Susan Kasen Summer and Robert D. Summer)

Salome, 1990, oil on canvas, 152.5 × 122CM, 60 × 48IN.

Sunset Song, 1990, oil on canvas, 203 × 218.5CM, 80 × 82IN.

Sabbath Vigil, 1990, oil on canvas, 203.2 × 218.5CM, 81½ × 87½IN.

Lovers, 1990, oil on canvas, 213.5 × 183CM, 84 × 72IN.

Berlin Wallflowers, 1989, oil on canvas, 218.5 × 213CM, 86 × 80IN.
(Collection Susan Kasen Summer and Robert D. Summer)

Vengeance, 1991,
oil on canvas, 152.5 × 172.5CM,
60 × 68IN.

Odalisque: Homage to R. & D., 1991,
oil on canvas, 218.5 × 203CM,
86 × 80IN.

Sabbath Ennui, 1991,
oil on canvas,
182 × 213.5CM, 72 × 84IN.

Lovers, 1991, oil on canvas,
152.5 × 152.5CM, 60 × 60IN.

Three Scottish Cousins, 1991,
oil on canvas, 152.5 × 172.5CM,
60 × 68IN.

My Grandmother, 1971,
oil on canvas, 172.5 × 172.5CM,
68 × 68IN.

Cockenzie, 1991,
oil on canvas, 203 × 213CM, 80 × 84IN.

Cockenzie Idyll, 1991,
oil on canvas, 203 × 213CM,
80 × 84IN.

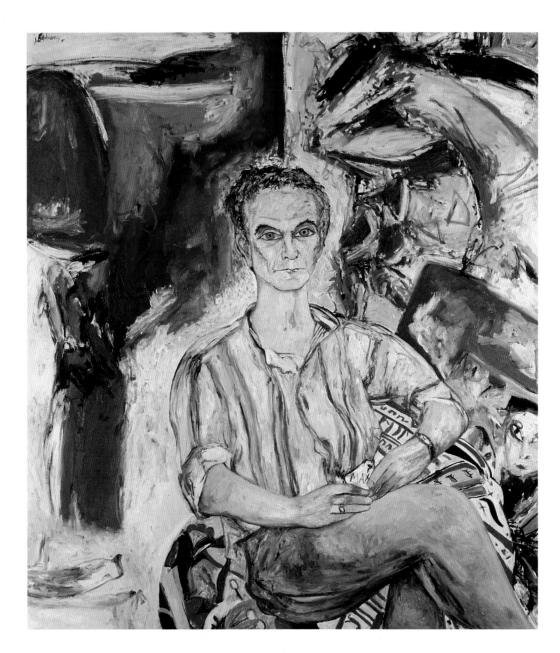

Peter Maxwell Davies, 1991, oil on canvas, 73 × 52.5CM, 68 × 60IN.
(Scottish National Portrait Gallery)

Prague Easter, 1992,
oil on canvas, 203 × 244CM,
80 × 96IN.

The Fortune Teller, 1992,
oil on canvas, 152.5 × 152.5CM,
60 × 60IN.

Cockenzie Fish Gutters, 1992, oil on canvas, 203 × 244CM, 80 × 96IN.

Margaret, 1992,
oil on canvas, 122 × 91.5CM,
48 × 36IN.

Self-Portrait at 50, 1992,
oil on canvas, 172.5 × 152.5CM,
68 × 60IN.

You're 50 Today, John, 1992, oil on canvas, 172.5 × 152.5CM, 68 × 60IN.

Budapest, 1992, oil on canvas, 152.5 × 152.5CM, 60 × 60IN.

Dresden, 1992,
oil on canvas, 122 × 122CM,
48 × 48IN.

The Sword Swallower of Prague, 1992,
oil on canvas, 152.5 × 152.5 CM,
60 × 60IN.

The Old Woman of Budapest, 1992,
oil on canvas, 172.5 × 152.5CM,
68 × 60IN.

Homage to Budapest, 1992, oil on canvas (triptych), 172.5 × 304CM, 68 × 120IN.

Goodnight Vienna, 1992, oil on canvas, 177.5 × 203CM, 70 × 80IN.

Danse Macabre, 1993, oil on canvas, 214 × 366CM.

The Storm, 1991, 190.5 × 253CM, 75 × 99½IN.

The Two Sisters, 1993,
oil on canvas, 152.5 × 172.5CM,
60 × 68IN.

The Girl and the Screeching Gannet, 1993,
oil on canvas, 91.5 × 91.5CM,
36 × 36IN.

Scottish Widow, 1992,
oil on canvas, 152.5 × 122CM,
60 × 48IN.

Bounteous Sea, 1993, oil on canvas (triptych), 212 × 366CM.

Sisters, 1993,
oil on canvas, 172.5 × 152.5CM,
68 × 60IN.

Homage to Lorca, 1993,
oil on canvas, 152.5 × 152.5CM,
60 × 60IN.

Charon's Boat, 1993,
oil on canvas, 172.5 × 172.5CM,
68 × 68IN.

Haunted Soul, 1993,
oil on canvas, 122 × 91.5CM,
48 × 36IN.

Woman of the North Sea, 1994,
oil on canvas, 121.5 × 91.5CM, 48 × 36IN.

The Conjurer, 1993, oil on canvas (triptych), 172.5 × 307CM, 68 × 124¾IN.

Homage to Rimbaud, 1993, watercolour on paper, 76.5 × 57CM, 30 × 22½IN.

The Journey, 1993, watercolour on paper, 76 × 58.5CM, 30 × 23IN.

Enigma, 1993, watercolour on paper, 57 × 76CM, 22 × 30IN.

Lovers by the Sea, 1993, 172.5 × 172.5CM, 68 × 68IN.

Elegy, 1993, 183 × 244CM, 72 × 96IN.

Black Dog, 1994, oil on canvas, 127 × 102CM, 50 × 40IN.

Birthday Self-Portrait, 1993, oil on canvas, 203 × 178CM, 80 × 70IN.

Sentinel, 1994, oil on canvas, 203 × 178CM, 80 × 70IN.

The Piano, 1994, oil on canvas, 203 × 178CM, 80 × 70IN.

Meeting of the North Sea People, 1994, oil on canvas, 203 × 178CM, 80 × 70IN.

Portrait of Sarah, 1989, oil on canvas, 122 × 152.5CM, 48 × 60IN. (Fitzwilliam Museum, University of Cambridge)

Eckehardt Schall, 1987,
oil on canvas, 172.5 × 152.5CM,
68 × 60IN.

Confrontation, 1994, oil on canvas, 203 × 178CM, 80 × 70IN.

Interior Thoughts, 1994, oil on canvas, 203 × 178CM, 80 × 70IN.

The Celtic Albatross, 1993, oil on canvas (triptych), 172.5 × 307CM, 68 × 124¾IN.

John and Helen Bellany, Edinburgh, 1992

Previous page: The wall of John
Bellany's room at Addenbrooke's
Hospital

Epilogue

John Bellany's achievement as an artist received its fullest official recognition when he was appointed a Commander of the British Empire in the sovereign's New Year's Honours List 1994. It gave him great pleasure, perhaps most of all because of what it meant to his family and friends, especially in Port Seton and Eyemouth.

There were many letters of congratulation, including one which congratulated Helen on being the greater woman who lies behind every great man's success. The numerous portraits of Helen are the artist's witness to that, as much as his Jonah-like deliverance.

Nothing could be more indicative of his return to health than the day we reviewed the paintings in the Cambridge studio. For six hours he moved canvases, working his way through the stacks, hanging each painting, whatever the size, meticulously straight for us to judge. Many were from the series on Eastern Europe. It was amazing to think he had completed them in the last two years. 'John's quite hopeless about practical things. He only really likes painting,' said Helen, whose view he denied, though even that day he had taken himself off to the studio at 3 a.m. He paints as much by night as day, not always successfully. 'This one's reportage,' he said of a conventional view of Eyemouth harbour done following our visit in the winter. 'I like to go back to basics from time to time; but it's not for the book. There's a difference between reportage and image-making. Here's one I did to cheer myself up!' It was of the Blue Bonnets in full swing. 'It did too!'

A portrait of Terry Waite, done shortly after his long ordeal as a hostage in Beirut, passed by. Waite had read aloud the typescript of his book *Taken on Trust* while John painted. A 1967 painting appeared, *Pourquoi?*, a bowed figure in front of a cross in the shape of a 'Y', one of his most dramatic from the period of the Holocaust pictures, followed by what he approvingly calls 'beezers' – the best, paintings 'with meat on the bone': *Wild Thyme*, as wild in colour as in spirit, a whole career away from the subdued and earthy *Pourquoi?* Superb. *The Bride and Time*, so rich in colour and spatially audacious, the design encompassing several different spaces, with an hour-glass floating free, symbolic of his own renewal; *The*

Girl with her pet, Buckie

Wanton Bride, a title good enough for a boat; and *Amaranth*, which is a boat.

This last is a haunting picture: the gabled east-coast houses, the red and blue boat and, in the foreground, a spectral group marooned on a bed with the sea flooding in. I think of it as I write this. Thirty-two years ago almost to the day I was driving to Eyemouth to fetch the district nurse. She would check on my father, who was convalescing after a heart attack. A sea haar had turned the land ghostly and set the coastal fog-horns booming. When my father died at lunchtime that day it was as if he had been gathered by the untold legions of the dead. In his art John Bellany has conveyed the feelings I have struggled to put into words so many times since then.

50th birthday photograph by Mike Tracey, 1992

Notes

1. The initials of a boat signify the first and last letters of its port of registration: for example, Port Seton boats are registered LH after Leith. Several of today's Port Seton skippers were at school with John Bellany, such as Peter Jarron, skipper of the *Star of Hope*. In the same way, he has known certain boats since his youth. As a boy, he painted a picture of the *Ebeneezer*, built at Weatherhead's yard at Port Seton, when 'there were just the timbers up'. Bellany's paternal uncles were all involved in fishing. The oldest, Uncle James, was a ship's chandler; the second, Uncle Bill, was skipper of the *Lothian Queen* and the *Estrelita* (South American Spanish for 'Little Star', 'he was a bit of a romancer') and the fourth in the family, Uncle John, fuelled the boats. Bellany's father was the fifth child of six. The day we visited Eyemouth there was one 'wreck' in the harbour from Ballantrae, old enough, John reckoned, 'to have been owned by The Master himself!'.

2. In his address as Director, Glasgow Museums, at the opening of 'A Long Night's Journey into Day: the Art of John Bellany', 9 July 1992.

3. Alexander Moffat, 'Our Apprenticeship Years', *John Bellany: Paintings, Watercolours and Drawings 1964–86*, Scottish National Gallery of Modern Art, Edinburgh, 1986, p.20.

4. 'Eyemouth is a scene of unutterable woe. Many families are bereft of husbands, fathers and brothers, while there is hardly one in the village who does not mourn the loss of some relative. The grief of those who bewail the dead, and the stony despair of the relatives of the missing ones, is terrible to witness, and the town is full of heartrending scenes.' From the *Berwickshire News*, 18 October 1881.

5. Alan Bold, 'John Bellany: a Portrait of the Artist', in *John Bellany: Paintings, Watercolours and Drawings 1964–86*, Scottish National Gallery of Modern Art, Edinburgh, 1986, p.30.

6. The Watchhouse's visual power is well described by Daniel McIver, a minister in Eyemouth in the first years of the century. Having described the building's 'weird and suggestive representations of what death does to the body', he adds a word of pastoral warning: 'Today the idea would be revolting to the average mind: men want to be reminded, not of what takes place with the body, but of that sphere to which the soul may go when life on earth is over.' James McKelvie, *An Old-Time Fishing Town: Eyemouth*, 1910, p.164.

7. The most important appearance of the Devil in the New Testament is in the story of Christ's temptation in the wilderness before he began his ministry. The most graphic account is in Luke, ch. 4 v. 1–13, from which I quote v. 5–8:

> 5. And the Devil taking him up into an high mountain, shewed unto him all the kingdom of the world in a moment of time.

> 6. And the Devil said unto him. All this power will I give thee, and the glory of them: for that is delivered unto me; and to whomsoever I will I give it.

> 7. If thou therefore wilt worship me, all shall be thine.

> 8. And Jesus answered and said unto him, Get thee behind me, Satan: for it is written, Thou shalt worship the Lord thy God, and him only shalt thou serve.

8. *Redemption Song Book*, 'Will Your Anchor Hold?', no. 180

9. Frances Spalding, *Dance Till the Stars Come Down*, Hodder & Stoughton, 1991, p.216.

10. Alan Bold, 'John Bellany: A Portrait of the Artist', in *John Bellany: Paintings, Watercolours and Drawings 1964–86*, Scottish National Gallery of Modern Art, Edinburgh, 1986, p.28.

11. Michael Horovitz, *Alan Davie*, Methuen, London, 1963, p.4 of Horovitz's text (the pages are un-numbered).

12. 'These two painters are declaredly "committed" (which is why they display their works al fresco), "political", "socialist realist". They reject the criteria and the social and political implications of the established academies and prefer to exhibit for all to see without let or hindrance or entrance fee.
'This is all, maybe, a bit by the way, for the paintings of Moffat and Bellany [*sic*] are of merit – as paintings. Aesthetically, their political message is no less and no more important than the political or social messages of Daumier or Rowlandson.
'As a painter, Bellany is a romantic; his protest is similar to that of Delacroix, who is living, for the moment, next door. Bellany [*sic*] is an artist of talent who has not yet found his direction.'
Sidney Goodsir Smith, *The Scotsman*, 23 August 1964.

13. 'How could we, as young artists, abandon this new tradition for an old one, without selling out our cherished belief in progress? Such a question might seem ridiculous in this so-called post-modernist era, but in the early 1960s it was a very real problem. We had run ahead of ourselves in adopting abstraction and this, combined with a growing social conscience, led directly to our first artistic crisis. I remember arguing that after Kandinsky, after Matisse, after Pollock, there was no way back, but eventually to break out from our formal straight-jacket we would simply have to go back and look again at the entire history of modern painting. Slowly, we began to admit to certain figurative

possibilities for our own painting, something which would have been inconceivable a few months previously.'

Alexander Moffat, op. cit., pp.19–20.

14. Among John Bellany's favourite paintings in the National Gallery of Scotland are those by Titian, Rubens and Rembrandt. He also particularly likes *Old Woman Cooking Eggs* by Velazquez, *Fabula* by El Greco and *Verdonck* by Frans Hals. His number-one favourite is Rembrandt's *Self-Portrait* (1657).

Over the years Bellany has assembled a 'top quality' Scottish collection. This includes major works by Orchardson, Ferguson, Hunter, Gillies, Colquhoun, MacBryde, Gear and Davie. He has two paintings by Gillies, on whom he contributed the following assessment for W. Gordon Smith's *W.G. Gillies, A Very Still Life* (Atelier Books, 1991):

'Willie Gillies did not believe in verbiage – he was "a man of the eye". Although he did not actually teach me I was constantly aware of his presence as Principal when I was a student at ECA. When not "office–bound" he was locked in his studio painting in his private domain. Only once was I allowed to enter the hallowed place and that was to help a janitor carry one of his paintings to a waiting van . . . He was popular and much loved and respected by everybody. He was part of the Auld Alliance between France and Scotland and continued this tradition, although after his initial sojourn in France he seemed seldom to have crossed Hadrian's Wall.

'He was in awe of the wonders of nature. He saw and portrayed nature tirelessly, with his own special freshness. He lived and breathed inside the landscape and with his alchemy could produce, from time to time, a masterpiece – sometimes with the innocence of a child and at other times with the sophistication of a sage. He was a "good artist".'

Bill Gear and Bellany drew and exchanged portraits of each other at the time of Bellany's Ikon show in Birmingham in 1982, a practice Bellany encourages 'because it brings artists closer to each other'. Gear's was 'a Matisse-like triptych, his first figurative drawing since 1952'.

Gear recalled Bellany arriving at his house 'bringing a bottle of vodka and a bottle of malt whisky - for lunch!' He added that *Ulysses and Calypso* by Max Beckmann painted in 1943, which he had seen in Berlin, 'looks to all intents and purposes like a John Bellany self-portrait'.

Bill Gear writes: 'Bellany, rejecting the traditional Edinburgh school of painting which had become cosy and inbred, turned away from the Paris-orientated picture-making recipe towards the untapped vein of German Expressionism, notably Max Beckmann.

'He wisely exploited his masterly gifts as a draughtsman and did not fall into the trap of facile abstraction. It is noteworthy that his concern for figuration was later on evident in the work of the younger Glasgow Boys.'

15. 'It is hard for younger people today to reconstruct the atmosphere of an institution like the National Galleries of Scotland 33 years ago, when the Gallery of Modern Art first opened its doors at Inverleith House in the Royal Botanic Garden. If we smile at the tartan trousers now decreed for the attendant staff, we should recall that, then, the doorman at the National Gallery had only recently given up wearing the uniform of cocked hat and cloak, said to have been modelled on the coachman's livery of a former Chairman of Trustees. But the Director still had an open fire in his office, fed and tended by the head attendant, who was the only intermediary between the public and the Director.'

Douglas Hall, *Curator's Tightrope*, an address to mark the publication of *The Concise Catalogue of the Scottish National Gallery of Modern Art*, November 1993.

It is also worth noting the change in the purchase grant over the years. From 1903 to 1953 the National Gallery and National Portrait Gallery received annual grants of £1,000 and £200, respectively. In 1960 the Gallery of Modern Art had an annual grant of £7,500. In 1986, when Douglas Hall retired, the grant was £650,000. In 1993 Miro's *Maternity* alone was bought for £1.5 million. In 1993 the collection numbered 4,500 items, most of it purchased or donated during Douglas Hall's enlightened keepership.

Bellany has been well served by Hall and by his successor, Richard Calvocoressi. His first work to enter the collection was *Mizpah* (1978), oil on canvas, in 1980. By 1994 the gallery had purchased a total of 7 oils, 12 original works on paper, 25 etchings and 3 portfolios (five prints apiece) with poems by Alan Bold.

16. Douglas Hall, foreword to *Kathleen Browne* by Marian Kratochwil, privately published, no date.

17. Hugh MacDiarmid, *Lucky Poet: a Self-Study in Literature and Political Ideas*, Jonathan Cape, 1972, p.320.

18. Alexander Moffat, op. cit., p.21.

19. Brian Sewell, 'Saving the Empty Hero' in *The Evening Standard*, 30 March 1989. Sewell criticised Bellany for repetition and found his acceptance of a liver to replace one destroyed by drink 'morally odious': 'As the pictures became more crassly confused and incompetent, pale and greasy, slick and degraded, so the critics promoted the painter as Britain's greatest living figurative artist – what unctious [*sic*] codswallop of praise for a fumbling hand, a fading eye and a fuddled brain. As his crippled liver drowned in the tide of alcohol, so painting ceased to be a profession and became a therapy.'

20. Alexander Moffat, op. cit., p.26.

21. Idem, p.23.

22. Idem, p.26.

23. The conversation took place in Bellany's studio at Windmill Drive. He was particularly impressed because Matta had been told the same thing by Matisse.

24. Keith Hartley, Introduction, *John Bellany: Paintings, Watercolours and Drawings 1964–86*, op. cit., p.13.

25. On Picasso's 90th birthday, which took place when Bellany was teaching at Winchester, John and his students made a celebratory poster and 'flooded the town with it'. He also organised lectures and events in Picasso's honour to mark the day, 11 November.

26. The image was inspired by Goya's *You who are unable* (Caprice 42) which shows two men carrying donkeys.

27. Eddie Wolfram, Introduction, in the catalogue for 'John Bellany', Drian Gallery, 25 September to 12 October 1973.

28. Job 10, 1.

29. Victor Musgrave, *John Bellany: Paintings 1972–1982*, Ikon Gallery, Birmingham, 1982.

30. Robin Gibson, Foreword, *John Bellany: New Portraits*, National Portrait Gallery, London, 1986.

31. Robin Gibson, op. cit., p.27.

32. 'The Way of the World', *The Daily Telegraph*, 24 January 1986.

33. From Joan Bakewell, *Heart of the Matter*, BBC TV 1989.

34. Idem.

35. Peter Fuller, Introduction, *John Bellany: Prints, Drawings and Watercolours 1970–1993*, Berkeley Square Gallery, 1993.

36. John McEwen, 'Son of the Sea' (with photograph by Snowdon), *Telegraph Magazine*, 19 May 1990.

37. Alexander Moffat, *A Long Day's Journey into Night: the Art of John Bellany*, Art Gallery and Museum, Kelvingrove, Glasgow, 1992, p.9.

On 26 August 1994 John Bellany officially opened the Port Seton Civic Centre and Library.

Biography

1942   Born in Port Seton, Scotland

1960–65   Edinburgh College of Art

Studied painting under Sir Robin Philipson

1965–68   Royal College of Art, London

Studied under Carel Weight and Peter de Francia

1967   Official cultural visit to East Germany with Alan Bold and Alexander Moffat: visited Dresden, Halle, Weimar, East Berlin and the Concentration Camp of Buchenwald

1968   Lecturer in Painting, Brighton College of Art

1969–73   Lecturer in Painting, Winchester College of Art. Visiting Lecturer at Royal College of Art and Goldsmiths College of Art

1978–84   Lecture in Painting, Goldsmiths College of Art

1983   Artist in Residence, Victoria College of the Arts, Melbourne, Australia

1988   Elected Fellow of Trinity Hall, Cambridge

1994   Awarded CBE by Her Majesty The Queen

AWARDS, COMMISSIONS AND PRIZES

1962   Andrew Grant Scholarship; travelled to Paris

1965   Postgraduate Travelling Scholarship; travelled to Holland and Belgium.

Commissioned by Ministry of Agriculture and Fisheries to paint murals for Chesser House, Edinburgh

1965   Burston Award at Royal College of Art

1980   John Moores Prize Winner

1981   Major Arts Council Award

1985   Athena International Art Award (joint first-prize winner)

1987   Wollaston Award, Royal Academy

1991   Commissioned to paint Lord Renfrew and Sir Roy Calne by the National Portrait Gallery, London

1992   British Council visit to Central Europe, Prague, Vienna, Budapest

1993   Korn/Ferry Picture of the Year, Royal Academy

PUBLIC COLLECTIONS

Aberdeen Art Gallery

Arts Council of Great Britain

Belfast Polytechnic

British Council

British Museum, London

Chesser House, Edinburgh

Contemporary Art Society

Dundee Central Museum and Art Gallery

Edinburgh Corporation

Ferens Art Gallery, Hull

Fitzwilliam Museum, Cambridge

Glasgow Art Galleries and Museums

Government Art Collections

Hatton Gallery, University of Newcastle-upon-Tyne

Hunterian Art Gallery, University of Glasgow

J.F. Kennedy Library, Boston

Kirkcaldy Museum and Art Gallery

Leeds City Art Gallery

Leicester Museum and Art Gallery

MacLaurin Art Gallery, Ayr

Metropolitan Museum of Art, New York

Middlesbrough Art Gallery

Museum of London

Museum of Modern Art, New York

National Gallery of Art, Gdansk

National Gallery of Poland, Warsaw

National Library of Congress, Washington

National Portrait Gallery, London

New York Public Library

Perth Museum and Art Gallery

Royal College of Art, London

Scottish Arts Council

Scottish National Gallery of Modern Art, Edinburgh

Scottish National Portrait Gallery, Edinburgh

Sheffield City Art Gallery

Southampton City Art Gallery

Swindon Museum and Art Gallery

Tate Gallery, London

University of Western Australia, Perth

Victoria and Albert Museum, London

Whitworth Art Gallery, Manchester

Wolverhampton Municipal Art Gallery and Museum

Zuider Zee Museum, Holland

RETROSPECTIVE EXHIBITIONS

1986   Scottish National Gallery of Modern Art, Edinburgh Serpentine Gallery, London

1988–89   Hamburger Kunsthalle and Museum am Ostwall, Dortmund

SOLO EXHIBITIONS

1965   Dromidaris Gallery, Holland

1968	Edinburgh College of Art
1969	Winchester School of Art
1970	Drian Gallery, London
	Hendricks Gallery, Dublin
1971	New 57 Gallery, Edinburgh
	Printmakers Workshop, Edinburgh
	Drian Gallery, London
1972	Royal College of Art, London
1973	Triad Arts Centre, Bishop's Stortford, Royal College of Art
	Edinburgh City Arts Centre
	Drian Gallery, London
1974	Drian Gallery, London
1975	Aberdeen City Art Gallery
1977	Acme Gallery, London
1978	Glasgow Print Studio
	Scottish Arts Council, Edinburgh
	Printmakers' Workshop, Edinburgh
	Crawford Arts Centre, St Andrews
1979	Glasgow Print Studio
	Third Eye Centre, Glasgow
	Southampton City Art Gallery
	Newcastle Polytechnic
	Glasgow Print Studio
1980	Acme Gallery, London
	Moira Kelly Fine Art, London
1981	Goldsmiths College, London
1982	Rosa Esman Gallery, New York
1983	'Paintings 1971–82', touring exhibition to Ikon Gallery, Birmingham; Graves Art Gallery, Sheffield; Third Eye Centre, Glasgow; Rochdale Art Gallery; Hatton Gallery, Newcastle-upon-Tyne; Walker Art Gallery, Liverpool; MacLaurin Art Gallery, Ayr; Rosa Esman Gallery, New York; Christine Abrahams Gallery, Melbourne
1984	Dusseldorf Gallery, Perth
	Roslyn Oxley Gallery, Sydney
	Pier Arts Centre, Stromness, Orkney
	Mercury Gallery, Edinburgh
	Rosa Esman Gallery, New York
1986	National Portrait Gallery, London
	Fischer Fine Art, London
	Galerie Krikhaar, Amsterdam
	Inaugural Exhibition for opening of Henry Moore Gallery, Royal College of Art, London
1987	The Peacock Gallery, Aberdeen
	Nigel Greenwood Gallery, London
	'"The Old Man and the Sea" Painting and Prints', Compass Gallery, Glasgow
	Greenhill Galleries, Perth
	Roslyn Oxley Gallery, Sydney
	Butler Gallery, Kilkenny Castle, Ireland
	Hendricks Gallery, Dublin
	MacLaurin Gallery, Ayr
	'Bellany as Printmaker 1965–1985', Third Eye Centre,

	Glasgow; Printmakers' Workshop, Edinburgh; Aberdeen Art Gallery; Beaux Arts, Bath
	'Recent Acquisitions', National Portrait Gallery, London
1988	Ruth Siegel Gallery, New York
	Workshop Gallery, Edinburgh; Aberdeen Art Gallery; Beaux Arts Gallery, Bath
1989	'The Renaissance of John Bellany: Watercolours painted in Addenbrooke's Hospital, Cambridge'
	Scottish National Gallery of Modern Art, Edinburgh
	Fischer Fine Art, London
	'John Bellany – "A Renaissance"', Scottish National Gallery of Modern Art, Edinburgh
	Aberdeen Art Gallery
	Beaux Arts Gallery, Bath
1990	Raab Gallery, Berlin
	Ruth Siegel Gallery, New York
	Compass Gallery, Glasgow
1991	Fitzwilliam Museum, Cambridge
	Fischer Fine Art, London
1992	'A Long Night's Journey into Day – A 50th Birthday Tribute', Art Gallery and Museum, Kelvingrove
	'50th Birthday – A Celebration', Beaux Arts Gallery, Bath
1993	'Prints, Drawings and Watercolours 1970 – 1993' Berkeley Square Gallery, London
1994	Flowers East at London Fields, London

SELECTED GROUP EXHIBITIONS

1963	Edinburgh Festival Exhibition, hung on railings, Castle Terrace (with Alexander Moffat)
1965	'Young Contemporaries', London
	Edinburgh Festival Exhibition on Mound steps (with Alexander Moffat)
1966	'Young Contemporaries', London
1967	'Young Contemporaries', London
	'London Artists', Shrewsbury
	'John Moores Exhibition 6', Walker Art Gallery, Liverpool
1968	London Group
	'Twenty By Fifty-Seven', New 57 Gallery, Edinburgh
1970	The Nude, New 57 Gallery
	'Twenty By Fifty-Seven', New 57 Gallery, Edinburgh
	London Group
1971	Arcadia Fine Art, Edinburgh (with William Crozier; Rodick Carmichael and Peter Stitt)
	'Scottish Realism', Scottish Arts Council Touring Exhibition
	'Twenty By Fifty-Seven', New 57 Gallery, Edinburgh
	'10 Scottish Printmakers', Sussex University
1972	'British Figurative Art', Nova London Gallery, Copenhagen
	'Scottish Artists' (Touring Exhibition by New 57 Gallery, Edinburgh)
	'15 Scottish Printmakers' (Touring Exhibition Nicholas Treadwell Gallery, London)
1973	'Fanfare for Europe', Drian Gallery

'Figures in the Landscape', Arts Council Touring Exhibition

'London Group', Whitechapel Art Gallery

1974   'A Choice Selection', Scottish Arts Council Gallery, Edinburgh

'British Painting '74', Hayward Gallery, London

'British Art '74', Germany (British Council Touring Exhibition)

'John Moores Exhibition 9', Walker Art Gallery, Liverpool

1975   '4 Scottish Realists', Fruitmarket Gallery, Edinburgh (with Neil Dallas Brown, Bill Gillon and Alexander Moffat)

'English and Scottish Painting '75', Fieldborne Galleries, London

1976   'John Moores Exhibition 10', Walker Art Gallery, Liverpool

1977   '25 Years of British Painting', Royal Academy, London

'Expressionism and Scottish Painting', Scottish Arts Council (touring exhibition)

'London Group', Royal College of Art Galleries, London

'Scottish Painting', Edinburgh College of Art

'British Painting', Nottingham Castle

1979   'Scottish Artists', Amos Anderson Gallery, Helsinki

Tate '79, Tate Gallery, London

'Independent Irish Artists Exhibition', Municipal Gallery of Modern Art, Dublin (with Bacon, Crozier and Freud representing Britain)

'British Painting', Oxford University

'The British Art Show', Mappin Art Gallery, Sheffield, and touring exhibition

1980   'John Moores Exhibition 12', Walker Art Gallery, Liverpool (Prize-Winner)

'British Art 1940–1980: The Arts Council Collection', Hayward Gallery, London

1981   National Portrait Gallery, London

'The Triptych', Ian Birksted Gallery

'Peter Moores Exhibition', Walker Art Gallery, Liverpool; Fruitmarket Gallery, Edinburgh; Goldsmiths College, London

'The Nude', Angela Flowers Gallery, London

'13 British Artists', British Council exhibition touring Germany

'Art and the Sea', touring exhibition

1982   'The Subjective Eye', touring exhibition

John Moores Exhibition 13, Walker Art Gallery, Liverpool

'Contemporay Choice, Serpentine Gallery, London

'Inner Worlds', Arts Council touring exhibition

'Drawing Towards Prints', Printmakers' Workshop, Edinburgh

1983   Municipal Gallery of Modern Art, Dublin

'Self-Portraits', Scottish Arts Council touring exhibition

1984   'Scottish Expressionism', Warwick Arts Trust, London

'The Hard-Won Image', Tate Gallery, London

'The British Art Show', touring exhibition

1985   'Athena International Awards', Mall Galleries London (joint first-prize)

'British Painting', Manchester City Art Gallery, Fine Art Society, Edinburgh

1986   'Man and Animals', Arts Council exhibition, Nottingham Castle

'Celtic Vision', touring exhibition opened Madrid

1987   'Scottish Painting 1954–87, 369 Gallery, Edinburgh; Warwick Arts Trust, London

Awarded George Walliston Prize for best work in Royal Academy, London

Represented Britain: 'Ljubljana Print Biennale', Yugoslavia, '2nd Triennale of European Engraving', Grada, Italy

'The Self-Portrait', selected by Edward Lucie-Smith and Sean Kelly, Artsite Gallery, Bath; Fischer Fine Art, London

'The Scottish Bestiary' (portfolio of prints touring exhibition), The Banqueting House, London

1988   'British Romantic Painting', touring exhibition opened Madrid

'The Royal College of Art Print Portfolio Exhibition', Victoria and Albert Museum, London

1989   'El Greco' Exhibition, National Gallery of Scotland, Edinburgh (guest artist)

'Eros in Albion' (House of Massaccio) Italy, British Council Exhibition

'British Figurative Painting', selected by Norbert Lynton

'Every Picture Tells a Story', British Council touring exhibition, Hong Kong, Singapore, Africa

'Scottish Paintings since 1900', Scottish National Gallery of Modern Art, Edinburgh; Barbican Art Gallery, London

1990   'Glasgow's Great Britain Art Show', McLellan Galleries, Glasgow

'The Compass Contribution', Tramway, Glasgow

'8 Scottish Printmakers', British Council touring exhibition, Singapore, Glasgow

'Turning the Century, The New Scottish Painting' (touring show), The Raab Gallery, London, Milan, Berlin, USA (Bellany, Howson, McFadyen)

'Scotland Creates', McLellan Galleries, Glasgow

1992   New British Art, Denmark, British Council Exhibition

'Modern Masters' Print Exhibition, Berkeley Square Gallery, London

1993   Scottish Painting, Flowers East, London

'Small is Beautiful Part XI: Homages', Flowers East

'Contemporary Trends in British Art', Hayward Gallery, London

'The Line of Tradition', Scotland

John Moores Exhibition 18, Walker Art Gallery, Liverpool

1994   'The Bigger Picture', McLellan Galleries, Glasgow

'After Redoute: Recent Flower Paintings, Drawings and Photographs', Flower East, London

Bibliography

1969	Edward Gage, 'Positive evidence of new Edinburgh School', *The Scotsman*, 4 September 1969
1970	Oswell Blakeston, *Art Review*, vol. 22, no. 9
	William Packer, *Art and Artists*, vol. 5, May 1970
1971	Alan Bold, catalogue essay, Drian Gallery, London
	Alan Bold, catalogue essay, *Scottish Realism*, Scottish Arts Council, touring exhibition
	Interview in *Scottish Realism* catalogue
	Cordelia Oliver, 'Scottish Realism', *The Guardian*, 14 May 1971
	Catalogue essay, group exhibition with William Crozier, Rodick Carmichael and Peter Stitt, Arcadia Fine Art
	Eddie Wolfram, *Art Review*, vol. 23, no. 17
	Oswell Blakeston, *Art Review*, vol. 23, no. 15
1973	Alan Bold, catalogue essay, Triad Regional Arts Centre, Bishops Stortford
	William Crozier and Eddie Wolfram, catalogue essay, Drian Gallery, London
	Eddie Wolfram, *Art Review*, no. 4, 24 February 1973
	Eddie Wolfram, *Art and Artists*, vol. 8, September 1973
	Barbara Wright, *Art Review*, no. 20, 8 October 1973
1975	Alan Bold, catalogue esaay, 'Group Exhibition: John Bellany, Neil Dallas Brown, Bill Gillion, Alexander Moffat', Fruitmarket Gallery, Edinburgh
1977	Alan Bold, catalogue essay, Acme Gallery, London
1978	Martin Green, 'John Bellany: Paintings', *Art Monthly*, no. 14, February 1978
	Felix McCullough, *Art Review*, no. 5, 17 March 1978
	Simon Vaughan Winter, *Artscribe*, no. 10, January 1978
	Marina Vaizey, *The Times*, 8 January 1978
1979	Felix McCullough, 'Edinburgh Festival 1979', *Art Review*, no. 17, 31 August 1979
1980	William Packer, catalogue essay, Acme Gallery, London
	Lucy Ellman, *Art Review*, no. 12, 20 June 1980
	John Roberts, *Artscribe*, no. 24, August 1980
	Stuart Morgan, *Art Forum*, April 1980
	Marina Vaizey, *The Times*, 22 June 1980
1980	Heather Waddell, 'The Painter's Inheritance', *Glasgow Herald*, 14 June 1980
1981	Mary Rose Beaumont, *Art Review*, 5 June 1981
	Mike Von Joel, 'Profile on John Bellany', *Artline*
	Edward Lucie-Smith, *Artscribe*, no. 27, February 1981
	Mary Rose Beaumont, 'The Language of Allegory', *Art and Artists*, no. 181, October 1981

	Edward Lucie-Smith, 'Peter Moores Liverpool Project 6'
	Mary Rose Beaumont, *Art and Artist*, no. 183, December 1981
1982	Monica Petzal, 'British Artists – An Exhibition About Painting?'
	Edward Lucie-Smith, *Art International*, vol. 25/3–4, March/April 1982
1983	John Bellany, Paintings 1972–1982 exhibition catalogue Ikon Gallery, Birmingham (and subsequent tour)
	Victor Musgrave and Phillip Rawson, catalogue essays
	'The Voyage of John Bellany: A Triptych', by Alan Bold
	Robert Ayres, *Studio International*, vol. 196, no. 1001
	Peter Fuller, *Art Monthly*, no. 65, April 1983
	Irene McManus, 'Vision from the outer edge', *The Guardian*, 8 March 1983
	John Fowler, 'Bellany goes to extremes to reflect the hard life', *Glasgow Herald*, 7 June 1983
	Rasaad Jamie, 'John Bellany at the Ikon', *Artscribe*, no. 40, April 1983
	William Packer, *Artline*, no. 6
	Marina Vaizey, *The Times*, 20 March 1983
	Glasgow Herald, 9 June 1983
	Mary Rose Beaumont, *Art Review*, October 1983
	James Burr, *Apollo*, no. 117, May 1983
1984	Alexander Moffat, catalogue essay, Pier Arts Centre, Stromness
	Art Monthly, no. 79
	Felix McCullough, *Arts Review*, August 1984
	'John Bellany in Australia: A conversation with Jeff Makin', *Studio International*, vol. 197, no. 1005
	The British Council Collection 1934–1984 catalogue, reproduced *L'Horlage*, introduction by Julian Andrews, Director, Fine Arts Department
	Max Wykes-Joyce, *Art and Artists*, vol. 215, August 1984
	The Times, 21 August 1984
1985	Max Wykes-Joyce, *Art Review*, 11 October 1985
	Clare Henry, *Glasgow Herald*, 26 March 1985
	Hugh Clayton, 'Athena takes a leaf out of Booker's Books', *The Times*, 4 September 1985
	Gerrit Henry, 'John Bellany at Rosa Esman', *Art in America*, no. 73, March 1985
	'One City, A Patron', British Art of the 20th Century from the collection of Southampton Art Gallery
1986	William Packer and Robin Gibson, catalogue essays, *John*

Bellany: New Portraits, National Portrait Gallery, London

Richard Cork, 'Bellany's Voyage', catalogue essay, Fischer Fine Art, London

Alistair Hicks, *The Times*, 25 March 1986

Clare Henry, *'Personal view of Botham the folk hero'*, *Glasgow Herald*, 28 January 1986

Giles Auty, 'Fish Philosopher', *The Spectator*, 8 March 1986

Richard Cork, *The Listener*, 13 March 1986

Frances Spalding, 'British Art Since 1900'

Catalogue for Christies Auction, London and New York, reproduced *Southern Cross*, Newhart New World, 22 April 1986

Illustrated Catalogue of Acquisitions, 1982–84, Tate Gallery, reproduced *Death Knell for John Knox*, 1972 and *Janus*, 1982

Celtic Vision, introduction by Denis Bowen and Derrick Culley, June 1986

Christopher Johnstone, *Fifty Twentieth-Century Artists in the Scottish National Gallery*, introduction by Douglas Hall

Ninth British International Print Bienniale, March 1986

John Bellany illustrated catalogue, (Retrospective Exhibition) — Paintings, Drawings and Watercolours

1964–86 Scottish National Gallery of Modern Art Edinburgh and the Serpentine Gallery, London, preface by Douglas Hall, introduction by Keith Hartley

Alexander Moffat, 'Our Apprenticeship Years'

Alan Bold 'John Bellany: A Portrait of the Artist'.

'The Voyage of John Bellany. A Tryptich', poem by Alan Bold, Trustees of the Scottish National Gallery of Modern Art 1986

Clare Henry, *Glasgow Herald*, 12 August 1986

John Fowler, 'Profile on John Bellany', *Glasgow Herald*, 14 August 1986

John Russell Taylor, 'Bellany Wins a Titanic Struggle',

John Bellany Retrospective Exhibition, Scottish National Gallery of Modern Art, Edinburgh Festival, *The Times*, 12 August 1986

Mary Rose Beaumont, *The Financial Times*, 12 August 1986

'A Feast of Freshness', *The Sunday Telegraph*, 10 August 1986

Edward Gage, 'A Voyage to Hell and Back', *The Scotsman*, 12 August 1986

Waldemar Januszczak, 'Edge of Darkness and Beyond', *The Guardian*, 14 August 1986

Alistair Hicks, 'Academics Denied', *The Times*, 25 March 1986

Marina Vaizey, 'Hot Scots', *The Sunday Times*, 17 August 1986

Giles Auty, *The Spectator*, 16 August 1986

Terence Mullaly, *The Daily Telegraph*, 25 August 1986

William Feaver, *The Observer*, 24 August 1986

Edward Gage, 'Face to Face with Bellany', *The Scotsman*, 8 September 1986

Peter Jones, 'Bellany's Glowing Summer', *The Scotsman*, 28 October 1986

Alistair Hicks, 'New Scottish Colourists', *Vogue*, October 1986

John Bellany Retrospective Exhibition, Scottish National Gallery and the Serpentine Gallery, *Studio International*, Winter issue 1986

1987   *Trienniale Europea Dell Incisione* catalogue, Grado, Italy

William Feaver, *The Observer*, 7 June 1987

Waldemar Januszczak, 'Rare Thrills Among the Royal Academy's Conformity', *The Guardian*, 8 June 1987

Brian Fallon, *The Irish Times*, 31 August 1987

Dorothy Walker, 'Bellany at Kilkenny Castle', *The Irish Independent*, 29 August 1987

John Hutchinson, 'Flower of Scotland', *Sunday Press*, 6 September 1987

Aidan Dunne, *Sunday Tribune*, 30 August 1987

Bienniale of Graphic Art, catalogue, Ljubiljana, Yugoslavia

'The Whitechapel Auction, Whitechapel Art Gallery, London', *Sotheby's Catalogue*, 1 July 1987

Sarah Howell, 'Artist Face to Face', *Observer Colour Supplement*, 13 September 1987

Sean Kelly and Edward Lucie-Smith, *The Self-Portrait: A Modern View* (Sarema Press)

'Bakewell's View', *The Sunday Times*, 27 December 1987

1988   Ellen Lee Klein, 'John Bellany', *Arts Magazine*, April 1988

Alistair Hicks, catalogue introduction, Ruth Siegel Gallery, New York

Thomas Schnurmacher, *The Gazette*, Montreal, 6 April 1988

Edward Gage, 'A Voyage to Hell and Back', *The Scotsman*, 12 August 1988

Paul Huxley (ed.), *Exhibition Road – Painters at the Royal College of Art* (Phaidon Press), 1988

1989   Sarah Jane Checkland, 'Prometheus Restored', *The Times*, 22 March 1989

Clare Henry, 'Portrait of the Artist as a Patient at Death's Door', *Glasgow Herald*, 24 March 1989

Alan Bold, 'View from a Visionary', *Observer Scotland*, 26 March 1989

Alistair Hicks, 'Survivors and Debtors', *The Times*, 4 April 1989

Peter Fuller, 'New Liver, New Life', *The Sunday Telegraph*, 9 April 1989

Alan Bold, 'John Bellany Painting on the Edge', *Modern Painters*, Spring 1989

Mike von Joel, 'A to B and Back Again', *Artline*, vol. 4, no. 5, February/March 1989

Clare Flowers, 'Back from the Brink', *Scotland on Sunday*, 19 March 1989

1990   William Packer, 'Turning Point', *Royal Academy* magazine, no. 26, Spring 1990

William Hardie, *Scottish Painting: 1837 to the Present*

Duncan MacMillan, *Scottish Art 1460–1990.*

Peter Fuller, catalogue introduction, Compass Gallery, Glasgow

Edward Lucie-Smith, catalgue introduction, Ruth Siegel Gallery, New York

Peter Fuller, catalogue introduction, Raab Gallery, Berlin

John McEwen, 'Son of the Sea', *Telegraph Magazine*

1991   Jane Munro, 'John Bellany in Cambridge', catalogue introduction, Fitzwilliam Museum, Cambridge

Susan Pirnie, catalogue introduction, Highland Regional Council touring exhibition

Sister Wendy Beckett, 'The Rape of Titian', *Modern Painters*, vol. 4, no. 2

British Contemporary Art 1910–1990 – Eighty Years collecting by the Contemporary Art Society

1992   Ajay Close, 'The Art of Creation', *Scotland on Sunday*, 5 July 1992

Allen Wright, 'An Artist with Vibrant Good Hope', *The Scotsman*, 10 July 1992

Bill Hare, 'John Bellany', *Galleries Magazine*, July 1992

Robert Dawson Scott, 'Portrait of an Artist now Bursting with Life', *Sunday Times Scotland*, 12 July 1992

Miranda France, 'To The End of the Night', *The List*, 3–16 July 1992

Clare Henry, 'Vision of the Artist in Three Acts', *Glasgow Herald*, 13 July 1992

'Bellany's Day', *The Ticket*, July 1992

'Feature', *The Preview*, July/August/September 1992

Anne Simpson, 'A Portrait of My Love', *The Herald*, 28 July 1992

Tom Lubbock, 'Metaphorically Speaking', *The Independent on Sunday*, 2 August 1992

Andrew Gibbons-Williams, 'Back from his Brush with Death', *The Times*, 4 August 1992

Mary Rose Beaumont, 'Life, near-death, sin and wickedness', *The Financial Times*, 25 August 1992

Alexander Moffat, 'A Long Night's Journey into Day: The Art of John Bellany', catalogue essay, Art Gallery and Museum, Kelvingrove

'A Long Night's Journey into Day: The Art of John Bellany', *The Scotsman*, 18 July 1992

Keith Patrick, 'A Long Night's Journey into Day', *Contemporary Art Magazine*, Autumn 1992

1993   Sue Hubbard, 'Scottish Painters', *Time Out*, September 1993

'John Bellany', *Art Review*, October 1993

John Bellany, 'My Country Childhood', *Country Living*, October 1993

John Keenan, 'Pulse', *The Big Issue*, 19 October 1993

James Bustard, 'Revisiting the Trauma of Surgery', *The Scotsman*, 27 October 1993

Simon Corbin, 'John Bellany', *What's On*, 20 October 1993

John Moores Liverpool Exhibition 18, Walker Art Gallery, Liverpool exhibition catalogue

W. Gordon Smith, 'Painting the Town', *Scotland on Sunday*, 7 November 1993

Audrey Gillan, 'Bellany's Talent Recognised', *The Scotsman*, 31 December 1993

Bill Hare (ed.), *Contemporary Painting in Scotland*

Patrick Elliott, The Concise Catalogue of the Scottish National Gallery of Modern Art

1994   Richard Mowe, 'Yin the Picture', *Scotland on Sunday*, 9 January 1994

Maggie Barry, 'Billy's Been Framed . . . and the Big Yin Likes It', *Evening Times*, 20 January 1994

Alison Roberts, 'Under the influence of genius', *The Times*, 21 March 1994

FILMS AND DOCUMENTARIES

1975   BBC Television (Scotland): *John Bellany* directed by W. Gordon Smith (30 minute film)

1986   BBC Television *A Portrait: John Bellany* (15 minutes)

BBC Television *John Bellany, A Retrospective,* directed by Keith Alexander (30 minutes)

BBC *Heart of the Matter – John Bellany*, with Joan Bakewell (30 minutes)

1989   BBC *Heart of the Matter – 'Is Life worth Living? It Depends on the Liver'*

1991   TV *John Bellany* with Vivien Hamilton. (30 minute film)

1994   BBC2 *The Bigger Picture*

Index